LLOYD GEORGE'S

favourite recipes

JOHN JONES

Cover design by Elgan Davies, Welsh Books Council, Aberystwyth.
Drawings by David Griffiths.

ISBN 1 871083 75 3

Printed by Cambrian Printers, Aberystwyth
Distributed by The Welsh Books Council Distribution Centre, Llanbadarn,
Aberystwyth.

Published by John Jones Publishing Ltd, Borthwen, Wrexham Road, Ruthin,
Clwyd. LL15 1DA

LLOYD GEORGE'S FAVOURITE RECIPES

A Recipe Book

CONTENTS

Introduction

by

Mrs. Bobby Freeman

Most of the recipes in this booklet were complied, during the early part of the 20th century, by The Criccieth Women's Institute. They were first published, we think in 1919, as "The Criccieth Women's Institute Cookery Book; including Recipes for the Favourite Dishes of the Prime Minister (The Right Hon. D. Lloyd George, M.P.)"

One can imagine the excitement with which the ladies of Criccieth Women's Institute assembled this collection of recipes. It was first published when David Lloyd George was at the height of his turbulent career. He had led the country to victory in the War-to-end-Wars and was now Prime Minister in peacetime. A local hero to be honoured indeed, though we do not know whose inspiration it was to include a few of the Great Man's favourite dishes in the book. Nor, strangely, does anyone connected with the family now remember anything about the book's compilation.

We owe much to Women's Institutes. Collections of members' recipes, often old and treasured family favourites, continue to be unassumingly published, usually as fund-raising ventures; their worth often unrecognised until time reveals their importance. So it is with this little book. Though the Lloyd George 'favourites' give this collection a special appeal, the book is even more interesting because many of the recipes are so old. I suspect that many must have been taken straight from handwritten family cookery books still giving useful service to their owners - the granddaughters or even great-grand-daughters of their original authors. Though references to margarine and 'Bird's Egg Powder' appear here and there, on the whole there is little reflec-tion of early 20th century cookery in this book.

The little section of 'Real Old Welsh Recipes' is also interesting, as three of the four recipes, 'Brwas', 'Sican Gwyn' and 'Llymru' are from the very old days of what I like to call Welsh 'pastoral' cookery: that is, from the frugal life of the hill-farms. But the inclusion of 'egg powder' surely reveals a contem-porary war-time expedient. This section could in fact have been made larger as there are several more genuine Welsh recipes here and there throughout the book.

Now to the Lloyd George's 'favourites'. We are given five - but one he loved best was missing! It is now restored–see page 64.

Lloyd George adored cacen gri. Mrs. Blodwen Evans, who worked for the family for twenty-five years, lived in Criccieth. In her contented retirements she recaptured vivid memories of the great statesman's enthusiasm for simple, homely Welsh food. "How we loved a cacen gri!" she said. But only Dame Margaret could make it just the way he liked it! Mrs. Evans described how he would take a long walk in the afternoon, nearly always along the top road to Llanystumdwy, often coming home soaked to the skin. He would change into dry clothes, then come in to the fire. After a few minutes he would look at Dame Margaret and say, coaxingly: "Make me a cacen gri........!" And of course she always would.

"As she made them she used to plaster each one with plenty of butter and pile them on a plate, until they were absolutely soaking with the lovely Welsh farm butter - oh, how he used to enjoy that! Nobody could make a cacen gri like Dame Margaret!"

Lloyd George was also fond of pig's head brawn. Though there was a cook as well, he always insisted that Sarah the housekeeper made the brawn: ".....he simply couldn't bear anyone else to make that."

And with the mutton broth he loved would come a plate of oatcakes - the big, flat Welsh oatcakes curling up at the edges. A pile of them would be placed on the table - nobody else but he was allowed to cut them - and on the rare occasions when the family dined alone he loved to crumble these into his mutton broth in the old, Welsh country way: "How he enjoyed that!"

Lloyd George always retained his love of simple Welsh country food. Even when they entertained, which was often (when, I was assured, the table used to be 'absolutely gorgeous'), he would often have an omelet or just bacon and egg. On the other hand, Lloyd George liked his guests to have whatever they liked, and so it was usual for many dishes to be prepared. The dish of stuffed sole, Mrs. Evans is sure, would not have been one of his favourites, though she remembers it was prepared for guests. The fish he was fond of was salmon, and he had that often. He liked Welsh lamb, of course, and the local butcher kept Downing Street supplied.

Mrs. Evans went through this collection of recipes carefully and pointed out many in the main body of the book which she knew were also favourites of Lloyd George: Scotch Pancakes; Lemon Cheese Pudding; Ground Rice Souffle with Caramel Sauce "he adored that". He loved, too, Bread and Butter Pudding; Cabinet Pudding; the Iced Fruits (Mrs. Owens, who contributed this recipe, kept a confectioner's shop); Potato Cake and Short Bread; Orange Cake; Queen Cake; his sister-in-law's Date Cake; Blackberry and Apple Cheese; Gooseberry Jelly and Rhubarb Jelly.

Recipes for Cacen gri
        Pig's Head Brawn
        Steamed Snowdon Pudding
        Grilled Herrings   -
        Cheese Straws

supplied by Mrs. Evans especially for this book are given in the appendix.

B.F.
Cardiff

Mr. Lloyd George's Favourite Soup.

The white parts of eight or ten leeks, and four potatoes, three pints of milk, half a pint of white stock, a small piece of margarine. Method: Slice the potatoes and leeks very thin, put in a saucepan with two tablespoonfuls of water and a little salad oil or other fat. Simmer gently till tender. When quite soft pass through a wire sieve and add milk and stock. Pepper and salt to taste. The soup should not boil after the milk is added or it will curdle.

Mr. Lloyd George's Favourite Pudding.

1 lb flour, 1 lb raisins stoned, ½ lb suet, a pinch of salt, mix all together and moisten with milk. Put the mixture into a basin and boil for four hours. Serve with sauce or sugar.

Mr. Lloyd George's Favourite Tea Cake.

½ lb flour, 1 oz butter, milk, one tablespoonful of sugar. Rub the butter into the flour, add the sugar. Mix with the milk into a stiff dough and roll into thin round cakes. Bake on a frying pan, turning them over so as to brown both sides. Serve hot buttered.

"Bara Brith" Currant Cake.

2 lbs flour, ½ lb butter, 1 lb Raisins, 1 lb Currants, ½ lb Lard, ¼ lb mixed peel, 1 lb sugar, three eggs, 1 packet baking powder, 1 nutmeg, ½ teaspoonful carbonate of soda, some milk. Method: Rub the butter and lard into the flour, add the other ingredients, mix with sufficient milk to make rather a stiff dough. Divide into two or three cake tins and bake in the oven.

Mrs. Lloyd George, Brynawelon.

Stuffed Sole.

1 medium sized Sole, 1 oz butter, half pint picked shrimps, 3 tablespoonfuls cold water, juice of half a lemon, and a little salt. Skin sole, remove fins and head, make and an incision along the back; fill the pocket with picked shrimps. Grease tin, lay on the sole, sprinkle well with salt, pour over a little water to keep it moist then add the lemon juice. Cover with buttered paper and bake for fifteen minutes.

Shrimp Sauce to cover same.

1 oz butter, 1 oz flour, ¾ pint milk or fish liquor, ¼ pint picked shrimps, a few drops of lemon juice, a little salt. Melt butter, stir flour into a paste, add gradually water or milk. Bring to a boil and boil 4 minutes. When it has boiled add the lemon juice

Mrs. Carey Evans.

SOUPS

Milk Soup.

Mix a little oatmeal and water and let it stand over night. Drain off the water and add more fresh water, mix well and let it stand again over night. Strain through a fine sieve, then boil the water and when it is boiling add to it a little milk. Serve it with toast.

Mrs. Jones, Caellobrith Terrace.

This is Bara Llaeth, an old Welsh recipe from the days of extreme poverty. The addition of a little milk was a great luxury.

Potato Soup.

Ingredients: 1 quarter water, ½ pint milk, 1 lb potatoes, 1 onion, 1 strip of celery, 1 oz butter, 1 tablespoonful of fine sago, salt and pepper. Method: Slice the potatoes, onion and celery, make the butter hot in a stewpan, add the vegetables, fry and cook until the butter is absorbed, stirred frequently to prevent them browning. Add the stock and simmer until the vegetables are tender. Rub through a fine sieve, return to the saucepan, add the milk and bring to the boil. Sprinkle in the sago, cook until transparent, add seasoning to taste.

Miss Claudia Evans.

Tomato Soup.

1 lb tomatoes, 1 small onion, ½ oz cornflour, 1 oz butter. Melt the butter in a saucepan, put in the sliced onion (not to brown). Add tomatoes and let it boil. Season, then put it through a hair sieve, and return to the pan, add the cornflour mixed with a little cold water. Stir it until it boils.

Miss Roberts, Gwynfryn Lodge.

Egyptian Puree.
(a delicious soup)

Ingredients: ½ lb red lentils, 2 onions, 2 outside sticks of celery, 1 oz of dripping or margarine, 1 quart of water or any stock, salt, pepper, ¾ pint of milk.

Method: Wash the lentils, peel and slice the onions, wash and cut up the celery, melt the fat in a saucepan, add the lentils and stir until they have absorbed the fat, add the onions, celery and stock, bring to a boil, then simmer until the lentils are soft, about ¾ hour. Rub all through a sieve, return to the pan with the milk, season well and stir until it boils. Serve with dice of fried bread. If too thick add more stock or milk.

Mrs. Pritchard Roberts, High Street.

Bone and Brown Soup.

Ingredients: 2 lbs fresh bones, 2 quarts water, 2 onions, 2 turnips, 2 carrots, 1 teaspoon salt. Method: Chop the bones up into small pieces, clean and cut the vegetables, put into saucepan with cold water and salt. Bring to a boil and skim and simmer gently for three hours. Strain and use for soup.

Miss Claudia Evans.

Lentil Soup.

Ingredients: 1 lb red lentils, 1 onion, 1 oz dripping, pepper and salt, 2 quarts water. Melt the fat in the saucepan, and stir in the lentils, cut the onion in slices, add the lentils, also add the water, pepper and salt. Let these boil together for about 20 minutes, until quite soft. Season again if necessary. Run through the sieve, return to the saucepan, and boil up again. Serve at once.

Mrs. Burnell, Parkia Terrace.

MEAT DISHES

Savoury Mould.

Take 1/2 lb sausages, remove the skin, ½ oz geletine dissolved in a little water. Some stock, or if none, an Oxo cube does as well, season lightly. Cook all together in a saucepan, then pour into a mould to set. Eat cold. Anything else, such as the remains of chicken, rabbit, etc. can be used instead of the sausage, and if convenient a hard boiled egg cut up and put in the bottom of the mould before pouring in the mixture is an improvement.

Miss Whitaker, Marine Crescent.

Babolia.

2 eggs, salt and pepper to taste, small teaspoonful of curry powder, 1 cup of milk, tablespoonful bread crumbs. Chop meat fine, beat up eggs well in basin, add salt, pepper, curry powder, breadcrumbs and chopped meat, then a cupful of milk. Grease a small pie dish well, and add a little lemon juice. Pour in mixture and bake in a moderate oven for about ½ hour. Turn out and serve with or without gravy.

Mrs. Janet Jones, 2, Pensingrig.

How to use up Cold Rabbit.

Joint the meat, beat up an egg, add a little nutmeg, pepper and salt, minced parsley and breadcrumbs. Dip meat into batter, sprinkle with crumbs, and fry a light brown. Thicken a little gravy, pour gravy round dish. Serve hot. Garnish with lemon and toast.

Mrs. Jonathan, Bodlondeb.

Curry.

Parboil vegetables, meat, onion, carrots, apples, potatoes, celery, beans, and any vegetables in season. Then cut up in discs or slices. Heat some dripping or lard in frying pan, and fry vegetables with meat until onion slightly browns. Heat some stock and mix one teaspoonful of curry powder, salt and pepper. Pour mixture over vegetables and mix together. Well boil rice and put round dish.

Miss S. Roberts, Coedmor, Pentrefelin.

Curry.

1 oz fat, ½ lb cold meat, one teaspoonful of curry powder, dessert spoonful Worcester or other sauce, 2 or 3 tablespoonfuls of milk, one apple or tomato, pepper and salt. Fry the onions in the fat until brown, then add the cold meat chopped up with the curry, etc. Add a little water and browning, with a little flour.

Mrs. Burnell, Parkia Terrace.

Egg Cutlets.

1 egg, 1 oz grated cheese, 1/2 oz breadcrumbs, a pinch of curry powder, cayenne and salt, 1/2 oz butter. Boil the egg hard, melt the butter and put it to the dry ingredients in a basin. Bind them with yolk of egg, and shape on a plate. Dip in egg breadcrumbs, and fry in fat a nice brown.

Miss Roberts, Gwynfryn Lodge.

Rice Cutlets.

¼ lb cooked rice, ½ lb meat minced, 1½ oz suet, ½ oz dripping, small piece of onion, pepper and salt, 2 tablespoonfuls breadcrumbs, 1 egg, crumbs and fat for frying. Boil the rice, mince the meat, chop the onion, and fry the onion in ½ oz fat. add meat, chopped suet, crumbs and rice. Season well. Turn on to a plate to cool, and make up in cutlets. Crumb and egg and fry them, and garnish with parsley.

Mrs. Goodwill, Station House.

Fish Cakes.

Remains of cold fish, 1 oz margarine, 1 oz flour, milk, 1 egg, ¼ lb potatoes, chopped parsley, anchovy sauce, pepper and salt. Break up the fish into flakes. Mix cold potatoes and fish into a bowl and add all ingredients. Make thick white sauce with flour, margarine and milk; add to fish and potatoes. Mix all together. When cool take small quantities of mixture and form into balls or cakes, egg and breadcrumb them and fry in boiling fat.

Miss Griffith, Brynderwen.

Rabbit or Chicken Pie.

2 tablespoonfuls of double cream, 3 or 4 fresh tomatoes (according to size) 1 oz macaroni, small quantity of grated cheese (Parmesan) cold chicken, either boiled or roasted, pepper and salt to taste. Heat the tomatoes, then press out the juice through a sieve, boil the macaroni, which should be cut in small pieces. Cut up the chicken into rather small pieces, if you have only a small quantity of it only use two tomatoes, grated cheese and chicken, mix together in a bowl with a spoon, pepper and salt. Prepare light puff paste and line a round tin with it. If wished a little vermicelli may be sprinkled on the bottom of the tine before the paste is put in. Put in the mixture, cover the top with paste, and bake in the oven. Serve very hot, with either brown or thick white sauce poured round but not over the pie.

Miss Moss, Caellobrith Lodge.

Brawn.

1 lb shin of beef, 1 cowhill, 2 quarts of water, salt and pepper to taste. Simmer till tender. When cold cut up very small and return to saucepan with as much liquor as liked. Put into basins and turn out.

Miss Gaynor Owen, Parkia Terrace.

Stuffed Potatoes.

Partly scoop the inside out of a few potatoes, put some sausage meat inside and bake in hot oven.

Miss A. Jones, Henlyn.

Potato Rolls.

Mash ½ lb cold boiled potatoes and 2 oz margarine or dripping, a little salt, and enough flour to make into a paste which can be rolled out. Cut into squares, and put in the middle of each a little chopped or minced and seasoned cold meat. Fold over and pinch together, and bake in a brisk oven for 15 minutes.

Mrs. Walter Jones, The Cottage.

Cold Spiced Beef.

6 lbs of salt flank of beef, mace, nutmeg, ginger, spice, 2 small onions, 4 bay leaves, 1 carrot, 1 stick of celery, bunch of sweet herbs and some meat glace. First take the bone out of the meat, and slit the salt meat into a long thin piece. Sprinkle with the chopped parsley and spices, roll up in a cloth, and tie securely with wide tape. Place the meat in a stewpan, add the vegetables, herbs and bay leaves, cover all with cold water, and let it just simmer, but on no account let it boil. Cook for five hours and when done, tie the cloth tighter and press between two boards under a heavy weight until cold. Then brush over with glace and garnish.

Miss E. Grifflths, 27, Marine Terrace.

Nice Liver Dish.

Put 2 tablespoonfuls of butter or margarine in a pan to get hot, and take thin nicely shaped pieces of liver and dip them in batter, then in breadcrumbs. Put these in the pan on slow heat, covering them with a tin and letting them cook gradually, taking care to turn each piece when sufficiently brown. Serve with good brown gravy slightly thickened.

Mrs. Owen, Llety.

The reference to batter may be confusing. It means 'dip in beaten egg'

Potted Chicken.

Ingredients; the remains of cold roast chicken, to every lb allow 3 oz of cooked ham, 4 oz of butter, nutmeg, salt and pepper, clarified butter. Method: Pass the chicken and ham 2 or 3 times through the mincing machine, or chop them finely. Then pound in a mortar until smooth, adding seasoning to taste, and the butter gradually. Rub through a fine wire sieve, press into small pots and cover the contents with clarified butter.

Miss J.W. Thomas, Cardigan House.

13

Risoto.

(can be made with fish or meat)

½ Ib minced fish or meat, ½ lb breadcrumbs, 2 oz butter or margarine, 2 cups of good stock. Simmer gently for two hours. When firm, put into a wet mould, turn out and serve with gravy. Some grated cheese is excellent with the fish recipe.

Mrs. Lewis, Llanystumdwy Rectory.

Sheeps Head Mould.

A good sized head, plotted if possible, if not skinned. Boil the head till the meat leaves the bones easily, then take it off the fire and leave till cold. Boil down the liquid to a pint. Cut the head up in small bits, slice the tongue, line the bottom of mould with hard boiled egg then a layer of meat, season well with black pepper and salt, and as you fill up pour the liquid over. Leave it standing in a cool place all night and it should turn out very firm.

Mrs. Benwell, Castle House.

Casserole of Beef and Beans.

Soak ½ pint haricot beans overnight. Next morning skin and then boil in salted water about 1 hour. Drain and place in the casserole, upon them lay a few slices of Spanish onion, then ¾ lb beef steak seasoned with salt and pepper. Next add remainder of beans and onion and a little of the bean liquor for gravy. Stand in a moderate oven over 1½ hours.

Miss Jones, Caerwylan.

A sturdy country casserole with a marked resemblance to the cassoulet of Toulouse in the Languedoc.

Galantine of Beef.

½ lb steak or veal, ½ lb ham or bacon, ½ teaspoonful dry mustard, 1 egg, 3 oz breadcrumbs, ½ teaspoonful pepper and salt to taste and a little nutmeg. Mince steak and ham finely through machine, add crumbs and seasoning, and egg well beaten, mix well. Make it to a thick roll, then tie in a floured cloth, boil for 2 hours, roll in breadcrumbs, let it stand till cold. It can be boiled in a mould, but requires more boiling.

Mrs. W.H. Williams, Manchester House.

Sausage Pudding.

Line a moderate sized pudding basin with good suet crust, retaining a portion for covering the basin, fill it with 1 lb of fresh pork sausages which have been scalded, and have had the skins removed, and pour over it a sauce made as follows: Mince an onion and fry it with three or four sage leaves in margarine till the onion begins to turn yellow. Dredge a dessert spoonful of flour over it, and pour upon it two or three tablespoonfuls of good stock. Stir the sauce over the fire till it boils, season with salt and cayenne, let it cool and strain it over the sausages. Cover the pudding with the pastry with which the dish was lined. Tie it in a pudding cloth, plunge it into boiling water, and boil quickly for 1½ hours. Turn it out on a hot dish and send brown gravy to table with it.

Mrs. Oldfield, Breeze Hill.

Boiled Sausage.

1 lb shin of beef, minced, 1 lb minced, ½ lb breadcrumbs, 1 egg, mace, pepper and salt to taste. Mix well together and boil for two hours. To be eaten cold.

Mrs. Owen, Llys Caradog.

Savoury Steak.

Ingredients: ½ lb steak, 1 onion, 2 small carrots, ½ a fairly sized swede, 1 small turnip, piece of celery, pinch of salt, and sprinkling of pepper. Stock one pint, (or water if unavailable) 3 large potatoes. Method: Clean the meat and fry till nicely browned in a frying pan, first of all cut in small pieces. Then place in a hot pot. Clean vegetables and cut in dice. Place with meat in the pot, add pepper and salt and pour stock over. Place cover on top, and put into a moderate oven to cook for two hours. If it seems to be absorbing liquid, pour little more water on it. It is delicious in cold weather and simply cooks itself.

Mrs. K.G. Roberts, Plymouth.

Beef Stew.

½ lb beef, cut in small pieces, 2 carrots, 2 turnips, 3 leeks, tablespoonful of oatmeal. Put 4 large potatoes, after it has boiled an hour, and any scraps of meat with the potatoes, 2 quarts of water, good pinch of salt.

Mrs. Thomas, Cefn Castell

VEGETABLES AND SAUCES

Whipped Potatoes.

Whip boiled potatoes to creamy lightness with a fork, beat in a little margarine, milk, pepper and salt, lastly the frothed white of an egg. Toss irregularly upon a dish. Set in oven two minutes to reheat, but do not let it colour.

Miss Evans, Henfaes.

Boston Baked Beans.

Soak ½ lb white haricot beans in water overnight, and then gently simmer them in salted water until they are just not broken. Pour off the water, and place them in a fireproof casserole. Pour a large tablespoonful of treacle in the middle of the beans, so that it does not touch the sides of the casserole, then cover with a layer of sliced onions, then sprinkle some dry mustard on the onions, and lay some slices of fat bacon over the top of all, tucking it well round the sides so that all is covered up. Pour in water to just cover the bacon, and bake in oven gently for some hours, not allowing it to dry up. This is a most most savoury dish, and can be warmed up again and again.

Mrs. Draper, Tan Lon.

Timbale of Green Peas a la Cumberland.

Boil ¼ lb spaghetti until it becomes tender. Procure a nice round basin in beehive form. Boil about one quart of tender peas, pass through a wire sieve, then beat up two eggs. Add the puree of peas to this. Season with pepper and salt, and 2 oz of butter. Pour all into a basin, cover, with a layer of spaghetti. Steam for 40 minutes, and serve with Bechamel sauce.

Mrs. Drage, Parciau.

An attractive idea, probably from an early 19th century 'Great House' cookery book. Useful for those who have a surplus of homegrown peas.

16

Boudins of Mushrooms.

Ten mushrooms, 2 tablespoonfuls of browned breadcrumbs, 1 tablespoonful of cream, 1 tablespoonful of lemon juice, 1 oz butter, 1 grain cayenne. Peel the six largest mushrooms, peel and chop very finely the remaining four. Place the chopped mushrooms in a basin, and add the lemon juice, cayenne and cream, season with salt and pepper and mix well. Put an equal quantity of this mixture into each large mushroom, and smooth with a knife. Sprinkle over each a portion of the browned crumbs, melt the butter in a small can, and pour an equal quantity on each. Place the mushrooms in a greased baking tin and cook in a brisk oven for ten minutes, and serve hot.

Miss Gladys Roe, High Street.

Tomato Sauce.

Bake 6 large tomatoes in the oven until they are quite soft. With a spoon take out the pulp and strain through a coarse cloth or a strainer to take out the seeds. Then add salt and cayenne pepper to taste, and as much vinegar as will make it the consistency of cream.

Miss Myra Morgan, Bron Eifion.

An old and excellent recipe from the early 1800's.

Horseradish Sauce without Cream.

Make a gill of thick white sauce (milk and flour), let to cool, then add grated horseradish, which has been steeped in vinegar for ten minutes.

Mrs. Evan Jones, Ymwlch.

Sauce.

1 quart vinegar, 2d. worth pickle spice, 4 tablespoonful treacle, 2 teaspoonful salt, 2 tablespoonful flour, 6 tablespoonful sugar, 2 teaspoonful mustard. Put the vinegar and spice in a pan and bring to a boil. Mix the other ingredients with a little vinegar, then pour into the boiling vinegar. Boil for 20 minutes then strain.

Anon.

Brown Mustard Sauce.
(To be served with fish)

1 ½ oz butter, 1 ½ oz flour, fried till a nice golden colour, then mix with pint stock. Stir till it boils, add the juice of a lemon, a little cayenne pepper, a teaspoonful of vinegar and a teaspoonful of mustard. Strain through a tammy and serve.

Mrs. Travers, Emu.

An unusual recommendation because this is the sauce normally associated with grilled meat, especially pigs' trotters (St. Menehould). The fashion of enlivening fish with a mustard sauce is, however,worth reviving.

PUDDINGS AND SWEETS.

Puddings.

Half pound flour, half pound raisins, ½ pint milk, 1 egg, ½ lb suet, good pinch salt, no sugar. Boil for two hours, serve it with a little sugar and a little butter.

Anon.

Scotch Pancakes.

Mix together in a basin 2 tablespoonful of flour, 1 tablespoonful superfine oatmeal, 1 level teaspoonful of sugar and saltspoonful of salt. Break an egg into a cavity formed in the centre, add a teacupful of sour cream and stir in gradually buttermilk or milk till the mixture is moist enough to beat. When well beaten and full of bubbles, sprinkle in a quarter of a teaspoonful of bicarbonate of soda, and ⅛ teaspoonful of cream of tartar. Have ready a hot greased griddle or strong frying pan, or a solid oven shelf, and pour on a full tablespoonful of the batter. When the consistency is right the batter spreads slowly in a round shape about 4 inches in diameter. The under side browns very quickly and should be at once turned by means of a knife, which may also be used to press lightly back any batter escaping during the process of turning

Mrs. Drage, Parciau.

An early version of the familiar Scotch Pancake or drop scone which became incorporated into Welsh cookery when Scottish workers came to Wales. Oatmeal was as commonly used in Scotland as in Wales in the old days.

Snow Pudding.

Two tablespoonfuls ground rice, 1 quart milk, 1½ tablespoonfuls of sugar, teaspoonful of salt. Boil the milk, less a little to mix the rice with. Mix this, and pour into the boiling milk and boil all together with the sugar and salt. Then add a piece of butter the size of a walnut, and pour into a mould.

Mrs. Browning, Pentrefelin.

Raspberry Jelly.

1 pint lemon jelly, 1 pint raspberry jelly, the whites of two eggs. Melt the jellies and put in different basins. When they have nearly set, well beat into each the white of one egg, until they become a pink and white froth. Pour one over the other in a glass dish. Serve with custard made with the yolks of the eggs, or whipped cream.

Mrs. Rowland, Bryntirion Terrace.

Rochester Pudding.

Take 4 oz flour, 1½ butter, 2 oz castor sugar, 1 teaspoonful baking powder, I/2 teacupful of milk, 1 egg. Rub the butter into the flour, add the dry ingredients. Beat the egg well, add the milk to the egg, make a well in the flour, pour the milk and egg, beat well together. Put two spoonsful of golden syrup in a basin, work all round basin, pour in the mixture, put a greased paper on the top, and steam for two hours. The treacle forms a sauce over the pudding when it is turned out.

Miss Maggies Jones, 1, Pensingrig.

An Inexpensive Christmas Pudding.

½ lb each breadcrumbs, flour, suet, currants, raisins, 2 oz candid peel, 2 oz syrup, 4 oz brown sugar, half teaspoonful nutmeg, a little mixed spice, 1 teaspoonful baking powder, 1 teaspoonful carbonate soda, pinch of salt and a little milk. Make crumbs from white part of bread, soak crust in cold water, squeeze as dry as possible, and beat with a fork, mix it with syrup and rather less than half pint of milk. Add the fruit cleaned, and the peel cut into small bits. Mix the flour, breadcrumbs, baking powder, soda, spices, salt and syrup. Stir together, put in greased pudding basins and cover with greased paper. Steam 7 hours, the longer these puddings cook the darker they become.

Mrs. Coates, Pensarn.

19

Patriotic Pudding.

¼ lb flour, 2 oz butter, 2 oz castor sugar, 1 egg, 2 large teaspoonfuls of milk, 1 large teaspoonfuls baking powder. Grease a basin and put a good layer of jam. Cream the butter, sugar and egg. Add flour, baking powder and milk. Pour on to the jam, and steam 1½ hours.

Miss Jones, Caerwylan.

It is difficult to associate this with food shortages in the War as the recipe as not particularly easy on butter, sugar and eggs. Possibly it derives from the 19th Century 'Military Pudding'.

Lemon Jam for Cheesecakes.

¼ lb butter, 1 lb loaf sugar, 6 eggs (the whites of two left out), grated rind of 2 lemons and juice three. Put the ingredients into a pan and let them simmer over a fire until the sugar is dissolved and begins to thicken to the consistency of honey. Then pour into jars, add when cold, tie down and keep in a cold place.

Mrs. Travers, Emu.

Lemon Cheese.

¼ lb margarine, ½ lb sugar, 2 eggs, 2 lemons. Put juice of lemons, margarine and sugar together in double saucepan; it must not boil. Beat the eggs and put them in, and keep turning all the time until it gets thick.

Mrs. Fowden Jones, Eisteddfa.

Lemon Cheese Pudding.

Line a pie dish with pastry. Spread a layer of lemon cheese, then cover thickly with breadcrumbs, another layer of cheese, and another of breadcrumbs. Make a custard of one pint of milk, 2 eggs and a little sugar. Pour it in and bake till browned.

Miss C.A. Rowlands, High Street.

Batter for Tarts instead of pastry.

Four tablespoonful of flour, 1½ tablespoonfuls margarine, half teaspoonful of carbonate soda, half teaspoonful cream of tartar, half cup or more milk. Make into rather stiff batter. Cook fruit first, then cover with batter, bake in quick oven.

Mrs. Coates, Pensarn.

Cocoa Nut Tarts.

1½ tablespoonfuls butter, same of castor sugar, 3 tablespoonfuls of coconut, 1 tablespoonfuls ground rice, 1 egg, half teaspoonful almond essence, and a pinch of baking powder. Beat butter and sugar to a cream, add eggs well beaten, then add all the other ingredients. Line some patty pans with pastry, put a little raspberry jam in each and a spoonful of the mixture on top. Bake a nice brown.

Mrs. Brooks, Wern Ddu.

Bread and Butter Pudding.

Place a layer of thin bread and butter on bottom of greased baking dish. Sprinkle over with currants, chopped suet, then a layer of bread and butter, currants, sugar and suet, until dish is ¾ full. Cover with milk, grate over a little nutmeg. Place in the oven till nicely browned. Time 50 minutes.

Gwen M. Hughes, Ynysgain Fawr.

Scotch Apple Cake.

Ingredients: ½ lb flour, ¼ lb butter, ¼ lb castor sugar, 1 egg, teaspoonful baking powder, cinnamon, 2 or 3 large apples. Mode: Rub the butter into flour, sugar, cinnamon and baking powder, all added together until it appears like breadcrumbs. Add the egg well beaten, keeping a little to brush over top. Add a little water if necessary. Work all into a nice stiff paste and divide into a small and a large portion. Line a tin with the larger half, rolling out the smaller piece for the top, full up with minced apples, sugar and a little mixed spice or a handful of currants. Put on lid and brush over with egg. Prick all over with egg. Prick all over with a fork and put in a fairly hot oven for ¾ hour.

Mrs. Owen, Llety.

Apple Amber Pudding.

Take four good sized apples, peel and core. Stew apples with sugar to taste and add lemon juice to flavour. Have one egg and its weight in flour and butter or margarine, and 2 oz sugar. Beat sugar and butter into a cream, add flour and egg well beaten, and add teaspoonful of baking powder. Place stewed apples in a pie dish and the mixture over it. Place in a quick oven to bake.

Mrs. Grifith, Railway Hotel.

Swiss Roll.

Ingredients: 3 eggs, 4 oz flour, 4 oz castor sugar, 1 teaspoonful of baking powder, 2 or 3 teaspoonfuls of warm jam. Method: Sieve the flour and baking powder. Whisk the eggs and sugar until creamy, stir the flour lightly in, turn into a buttered tin and bake in a hot oven. Turn out upside down on to a sugared paper. Spread on the jam and roll up firmly. Time: from 8 to 10 minutes to bake.

Mrs. Griffith, Railway Hotel.

Marmalade Pudding.

Beat 1 oz butter and 1 oz sugar to a cream, add yolk of one egg, 1 oz marmalade, 1½ oz flour, 1 teaspoonful of baking powder, then the white of egg whipped to a stiff froth. Put in a well buttered basin and steam for 1¾ hours.

Miss Gaynor Griffith, Bron Aber.

Potato Pudding.

½ lb potatoes mashed, ¼ lb butter, ¼ lb sugar, 2 eggs, half teaspoonful essence of lemon. Melt butter, whip eggs and add to batter and potatoes, beat well all together. Bake in a moderate oven for half an hour.

Lady Ellis Nanncy, Gwynfryn.

Manchester Pudding.

Half pint milk, 2 oz breadcrumbs. Let the milk boil, and stir the crumbs into it on the fire. Let it boil together. When cold add 4 eggs, leaving out 2 whites, and 2 oz butter. Line your dish with puff pastry, and cover the bottom with any kind of preserve, strawberry or raspberry. Then pour on the mixture and serve. If you omit the preserve use the grated rind of a lemon and sugar to taste. May be served hot or cold.

Miss Priestley, Trefan.

The butter should be beaten into the crumbs and milk together with the yolks of 2 eggs and lemon rind. This is to give the yellow colour associated with the pudding. The custardy mixture is poured over the preserve in the pastry shell and the whites then whisked and spread over the top; the whole then bakes in a very gentle oven.

Ground Rice Souffle and Caramel Sauce.

3 tablespoonfuls ground rice, 1 pint milk, 2 eggs, 2 oz sugar, 1 oz margarine. Boil ground rice in milk until thick, add margarine and sugar. When cool add the yolks of eggs, beat the mixture well. Beat the white of egg stiff. Boil sugar and water to make the caramel until a golden brown. Line mould quickly with caramel add whites of eggs to mixture. Put in mould, cover with greased paper, and steam half an hour. Turn out on a dish and serve quickly.

Miss Phoebe Griffith, Brynderwen.

While Creme Caramel is familiar enough, I have only come across one other milk pudding recipe with a caramel lining.

Ground Rice Pudding.

Set a pint of new milk on the fire, and when it is scalding hot stir into it 2 tablespoonfuls of ground rice mixed up with a quarter of a pint of cold milk. Keep it on the fire till it thickens but do not let it boil. Pour it into a basin to cool, stirring in gently ¼ lb butter. When cold add some sugar, a little nutmeg, and 4 eggs well beaten with some salt. Fry these in as little lard as possible of a nice light brown colour. Serve them up with sugar sifted over them, and with lemon or Seville orange cut and laid round the dish.

Mrs. Williams, Montrose.

Another old and interesting recipe. The author means that spoonfuls of the rice mixture should be fried.

Ground Rice Mould.

1¼ oz ground rice, half pint milk, strip of lemon rind, 1 oz sugar. Moisten rice with a little of the milk. Boil rest of milk with sugar and rind. When boiled remove rind and pour milk on the rice. Return to the pan and boil for ten minutes. Then pour into a wet mould, when quite cold turn out.

Mrs. Lloyd Owen, Bank House.

Ground Rice Puff.

Boil a breakfastcupful of ground rice on a moderate fire. When cooked the yolks of one or two well beaten eggs and a little sugar. Pour mixture into a buttered pie dish, bake till set. Beat white of eggs to a stiff froth, add a tablespoonful of raspberry jam to whites of eggs, and spread over pudding. Put back in oven till a golden brown. Serve at once.

Mrs. Elias, Bryn.

Essex Pudding.

4 oz sugar, 3 oz butter, 3 oz flour, 1 teaspoonful baking powder, 2 eggs, milk, jam or syrup. Beat butter and sugar to a cream, add flour gradually and the eggs well beaten, then enough milk to make it consistency of thick cream. Butter a mould, spread jam round it, pour in the mixture, and steam 1 ½ hours, or omit jam and pour it hot golden syrup.

Miss Gaynor Griffith, Bron Aber.

Louise Pudding.

½ lb breadcrumbs, 1/2 lb suet, 2 eggs, 2 oz sugar. A large cupful of boiled sago not added until cold. Mix all together and boil one hour.

Lady Ellis Nanney, Gwynfryn.

Military Pudding.

Ingredients: ½ lb finely chopped suet, ½ lb breadcrumbs, ½ lb gar, the finely grated rind and juice of a large lemon, 2 eggs. Method: Mix all the ingredients well together, turn into well buttered small cups and bake in a moderate oven for 3/4 of an hour. Serve with a suitable sauce. If preferred the puddings may be steamed for the same length of time.

Miss J. W. Thomas, Cardigan House.

A well-known 19th century recipe, which has an accompanying lemon sauce, typical of the period: Rub the rind of a lemon on some lumps of sugar, squeeze out and strain the juice, melt 1 oz butter in a saucepan, stir in 1 tablespoon of flour. When palest golden colour add a large wineglass of sherry, a wineglass of water and the strained lemon juice. Crush the lumps of sugar that were rubbed on the lemon and stir them into the sauce, which should be very sweet. When the above is well mixed and the sugar has melted, add the beaten yolks of 4 eggs, stir the sauce over a gentle heat until it thickens, then serve. Do not on any account allow it to boil or it will curdle, and be entirely spoiled. From: "English Recipes" by Sheila Hutchins, pub. by Methuen.

Sponge Pudding.

Beat 3 oz butter, and 3 oz castor sugar to a cream, add the yolk of one egg well beaten. Stir in lightly ¼ lb flour and one teaspoonful of baking powder. Beat the white of the egg to a staff froth and add to mixture, put into a dish and bake for ¾ hour. Turn out and serve with marmalade.

Miss Gaynor Griffith, Bron Aber.

Marrow Cream.

(Substitute for Lemon Cheese)

Prepare marrow for cooking, weigh, steam until tender and mash. To every pound of marrow weighed before cooking add ¾ lb of sugar, 2 lemons, rind and juice, 2 oz butter. Cook for an hour stirring all the time. Grate the lemon rind.

Miss Jonathan, Bodlondeb

Unusual and worth trying.

Sweet Omelette.

Two eggs, lump of butter, dessertspoonful of castor sugar, pinch of salt. You put the butter in an omelette pan, and let it melt, let it get quite hot. The salt rises to top, take a spoon and skim the froth that rises to the top. Separate the yolks from the whites, beat up the whites to a stiff froth, and beat up the yolks and put in the sugar. You can put in the salt with the whites, it helps them to beat up better. Mix the whites very lightly into the yolks with a fork or knife, have the butter quite hot in the pan before you put the omelette in, have a sheet of paper ready sprinkled with sugar to prevent it sticking, leave it on the fire until it sets, then put it in the oven, pan and all, for a few minutes to brown the top of the omelette. Put the knife across the middle at the back of it and turn it over, spread jam on it.

Miss E.C. Jones, Parkia Ucha.

Cabinet Pudding.

Sponge cakes, macaroons, ratafias and milk. Make the eggs and milk into a boiled custard. Take a basin well greased in which a few stoned raisins have been placed. Line the sides and bottom with sponge cakes sliced in two. Fill the interior with ratafias and macaroons, and add the custard when hot to fill the basin, add a little sugar to taste. Steam for two hours and serve hot with wine sauce.

Mrs. Price, Victoria House.

Pineapple Sponge.

Half tin pineapple, ½ oz gelatine, white of three eggs, 1½ oz castor sugar. Dissolve gelatine in syrup, which should be made up to half pint with water. Cut up pineapple. Beat whites to a stiff froth, add gelatine (cool), whisk till nearly setting. Add sugar and pineapple, and pile up in a glass dish, and leave to set in a cold place.

Mrs. Hugh Williams, Pentrefelin Vicarage.

Seabreese Pudding.

Three sponge cakes split and laid in a glass dish and pour 1 pint of any kind of jelly over them and stand till next morning. Break up into knobs and heap up in the centre of the dish. Pour over it one pint cold custard, add some whipped cream and serve. Enough for six people.

Miss Gaynor Owen, Parkia Terrace.

How we love to vary the trifle, which has been with us for so many centuries! This simple idea is a real foretaste of 20th century quick cookery.

Iced Fruits.

Take fine bunches of ripe currants on the stalk, dip them in gum arabic water or the white of egg well beaten. Dry them on a sieve, sift white sugar over and let them dry. They are very nice for dessert or the tea table. Grapes, cherries or plums may be done in the same way.

Mrs. Owen, Llys Caradog.

Cup Pudding.

1 breakfast cup of shredded suet, 1 breakfast cup of flour, 1 breakfastcup of breadcrumbs, 1 breakfastcup of sultana, raisins, one and a half teaspoonfuls of fine sugar, 1 teaspoon of carbonate of soda, a little grated nutmeg, a little grated lemon, rind, a pinch of salt, a beaten egg and a little milk. Mix all the dry ingredients well together, then add the beaten egg and milk. Put in a well greased basin, cover with a scalded and floured cloth. Steam for at least three hours. Serve with white sauce.

Mrs. W. Talmage Davies, Llys Owen.

Macaroon Tart.

Some short pastry and jam, 4 oz margarine, 4 oz sugar, 4 oz rolled oats and flavouring. Have ready a flat tin thinly lined with short pastry, add a thin layer of jam, then spread the mixture on smoothly, bake in a moderate oven.

Mrs. Walter Jones, The Cottage.

Parlour Pudding.

Slice a small loaf into a pan, and put into it ¼ lb of butter, pour half pint of scalding hot milk over it and let it stand uncovered. When cool work it fine with a spoon, then add three eggs well beaten, 3 oz sugar, a little grated nutmeg, a pinch of salt, ¼ lb currants washed and dried. Bake in well buttered saucers or patty pans three quarters of an hour. Turn out and serve with white wine sauce.

Mrs. Williams, Montrose.

A 19th Century recipe.

Egg Jelly.

Half ounce leaf gelatine, 5 oz loaf sugar, 2 lemons, 2 eggs, half pint water. Dissolve the gelatine in water then add the sugar and let that dissolve. Grate the lemon rind, take sugar and water off the fire and add the rind and juice. Put in the yolks well beaten, and place on fire again, and stir till it begins to thicken. Whip up the whites stiffly and add them to the jelly. Rinse a mould out with cold water, pour in jelly and turn out when set.

Mrs. Williams, Montrose.

A Beggar's Pudding.

Take any odd scraps of bread, cut them small and pour on them as much boiling water as will soak them well. Let it stand till the water is cool, and then press it out and mash the bread smooth with the back of a spoon. Supposing the quantity of this to be a quart, add to it half a teaspoonful of salt, two small teaspoons of ground ginger, some moist sugar, and ¾ lb of currants. Mix all well together, and lay it in a pan buttered. Flatten it down with a spoon and lay some pieces of butter on the top. Bake in a moderate oven and serve it hot. When cold it will turn out of the pan and cut into good plain cheesecakes

Mrs. Williams, Montrose.

Economy indeed! The spicy ginger would of course make it warming as well as enjoyable. There is a resemblance here to Bara Dwr (bread and water 'soak' of wheat-meal bread, boiling water, ginger and sugar, an old Welsh invalid food of little nourishment but light enough for weak constitutions).
Slices of cold, curranty, spicy bread pudding are still enjoyed today, and perhaps they could be regarded as a plain substitute for cheesecake.

Boiled Batter Pudding.

Half pound flour, 1 oz sugar, 2 eggs, ping of milk, pinch of salt, half teaspoonful baking powder, small lump of butter. Put the flour and salt through a sieve into the basin, make a well in the centre of the flour, put in the eggs (do not beat the eggs put them in whole), and mix this well with a little of the flour, then add half the milk stirring all the while. Beat for ten minutes or quarter hour with wooden spoon the back towards you. Then add the rest of the milk and mix well, put in sugar and butter, let the batter stand for two or three hours then put in the baking powder, mix very lightly, pour the batter into a greased basin, cover with a cloth, boil for an hour and a half. Serve with melted butter.

Miss E.C. Jones, Parkia Ucha.

17th century recipe books give instructions for batter pudding. This one is a later version. The essential thing is to serve and eat at one, as it collapses when cool and resembles leather when cold. Cold butter and brown sugar are an alternative accompaniment.

Southport Pudding.

Six oz breadcrumbs, six oz chopped suet, six oz chopped apples, 4 oz sugar, a little nutmeg, and half rind of lemon. Mix with one egg and little milk. Boil for two hours.

Mrs. Owen, Llys Caradog.

Fruit Sponge.

Fourteen sheets of gelatine dissolved in a pint of water, then add a sufficient quantity of sour syrup or fruit juice to colour it, and sweeten to your taste. When rather cool, beat it for an hour, until it becomes like a sponge. Put into a mould, and turn out. Served with whipped cream. Not beaten it makes a fruit mould.

Miss Priestley, Trefan.

Chocolate Blancmange.

Two tablespoonfuls of cornflour, 1 tablespoonful chocolate or cocoa, 2 table-spoonful of sugar, pinch of salt, 1 quart milk. Mix all the dry things together with a little cold milk. Boil the milk, then pour in the mixture. Boil ten minutes, put in a piece of butter and pour into a mould.

Mrs. Browning, Pentrefelin.

Chocolate Cream.

Take ¾ pint milk, place in saucepan with packet of Mexican Chocolate (¼) or one tablespoonful of chocolate powder or cocoa. When blended together pour on to two yolks of eggs previously mixed with dessertspoonful of corn-flour. Return mixture to pan, stirring all the while until thick, but do not allow to boil. When cold place in a dish, and whip up the whites of the two eggs and pile on top. Serve sponge fingers with the sweet. This is very nourishing and a great favourites with children.

Miss Edith J. Thomas, Mynydd Ednyfed.

Chocolate Mould.

One pint of milk, 3 oz of chocolate, half ounce gelatine, whipped cream. Heat the milk, add the chocolate, when cooled a little and the gelatine. Place away to set. Then decorate with cream and fruits.

Mrs. Cambriensis Williams, Eryldon.

Apple Charlotte.

1 lb apples, 4 oz sugar, slices of bread and butter, grated lemonrind. Peel and core the apples and stew with the sugar and lemon rind in very little water. Grease a pie dish well, line it with thin bread and butter. Put in a layer of the apple, then a piece of bread and butter and continue this until the dish is full. Cover with a piece of bread and butter and bake in a moderate oven for about half hour. Turn out on to a hot dish and serve with cream or custard. This is an excellent way of using up stale bread and butter.

Miss Marian P. Williams, The Eifion.

Jam Sauce with plain Suet Pudding.

To 2 tablespoonfuls jam add one gill boiling water. Keep hot until jam is dissolved.

Mrs. Bartleman, Ymwlch.

Helen Pudding.

2 teacupfuls of milk, 3 eggs, leave out white of one, 1 teacupful strong coffee, sugar to taste. Boil the milk, pour on to the eggs which have been well beaten, add the coffee and steam for 20 minutes. Serve cold in a glass dish.

Miss Moss, Caellobrith Lodge.

Economical Pudding.

5 tablespoonfuls of flour, 3 tablespoonfuls of suet, 2 tablespoonfuls of sugar, 1 tablespoonful of syrup. One teaspoonful of baking powder. Mix with milk and steam 2 ½ to 3 hours.

Mrs. Davies, Bron Eifion Lodge.

Lemon Creams.

Lay the thinly cut peel of two large lemons in half pint water overnight. Strain next day, and add the strained juice of the lemons to it. Add also the whites of three small eggs whisked to a froth and sugar to taste and a sheet or two of gelatine. Stir over a quick fire till it boils, and thickens, like custard. When nearly cold pour into custard glasses. Top up with whipped cream before serving. This is a good cold supper sweet, and can all be made the day before, as it keeps.

Mrs. Draper, Tan Lon.

A quickly made Pudding.

Cut two or three cakes in halves, line a mould with them have ready some stewed fruit, fill up the mould, cover with remainder of cakes. Press down with a plate and a weight. Turn out and serve with custard.

Mrs. Price, Victoria House.

Modwena Pudding.

6 oz suet, 6 oz breadcrumbs, 2 tablespoonfuls golden syrup, 1 egg, or one dessertspoonful Bird's Egg Powder, sultanas, 1 teacupful milk. Put all the ingredients in a basin, mixing these with the cup of warm milk. Grease a pudding basin, and steam the mixture for quite two hours. Serve with a sweet sauce.

Miss Moss, Caellobrith Lodge.

French Macaroons.

Line small tins with puff paste, put a little raspberry jam on the bottom, then on the top a good teaspoonful of the following mixture, 2 oz self raising flour, 1 oz lard, 1 oz sugar, mix well with a little milk or egg, then place a layer of puff paste, cover with icing sugar coloured with cochineal, put 4 bars of paste across, bake 15 minutes on the top shelf of a hot oven.

Mrs. Harlech Jones, Harlech View.

Prune Mould.

½ lb prune stewed well in water with lemon peel, put through a hair sieve, add sugar to taste and half ounce of gelatine. Serve with whipped cream.

Mrs. Griffiths, Talarfor.

Currant or Sultana Pancakes.

Ingredients: ½ lb flour, 2 eggs, pinch of salt, pinch of cream of tartar, 2 oz sugar, 2 oz sultanas, ¼ pint buttermilk. Method: make a well in centre of flour, break the eggs and separate the whites from yolks, beat both well separately, pour yolks into the flour, and add the dry ingredients and mix well, adding milk until a thick batter is made. Beat all well till bubbles appear on the top, then sprinkle in sultanas, mix in the whites of eggs. Fry in rounds. Sprinkle with sugar and serve hot.

Mrs. K.G. Roberts, Plymouth.

Stone Cream.

¾ gelatine to 1 quart of milk, made up with a gill of cream. Melt gelatine and put in cold milk, and then add cream and vanilla and sugar.

Miss Moss, Caellobrith Lodge.

This recipe originated in the 17th century when it was made with white wine and not vanilla. A little preserve was placed at the bottom of each individual glass into which the cream was poured and left to set for a day before serving.

Margarite Pudding.

One breakfastcupful of flour, 1 good teaspoonful of baking powder, 2 tablespoonful of sugar, 1 egg, 2 oz butter or margarine, a little milk, grated rind of lemon. Well butter a mould and line it with jam, pour in the mixture and steam for 1 ½ hours.

Miss Gaynor Owen, Parkia Terrace .

Delicious Cold Pudding.

Two large tablespoonfuls of small sago, one pint of water, two tablespoonfuls of golden syrup, rind and juice of two lemons. When the water boils sprinkle in the sago, let cook till quite clear and thick, then stir in the golden syrup, lemon peel and juice, stir well together, pour into a mould which has been rinsed in cold water, leave to set, turn out and serve with custard or any stewed fruit.

Miss S.A. Jones, Tyn Gate.

Almond Tarts.

Line some patty pans with good short crust pastry, and put a small portion of raspberry jam in the centre of each. Then make the following mixture: 3 oz margarine creamed with 3 oz castor sugar, well flavoured with essence of almond, and stir in 3 oz ground rice, and one egg well beaten. Put two teaspoonfuls of mixture in each lined pan and bake in a moderate oven. These are delicious served as a sweet with custard.

Mrs. E. Jones, Highgate, Llanystumdwy.

Almond Tarts.

Line small tins with short paste, put in little jam on the bottom, cover with a good teaspoonful of the following mixture. Two oz of self-raising flour, 2 oz sugar, ¼ oz ground almonds, ¼ oz margarine. Rub in and mix to a thick cream with milk. Bake 15 minutes. When done ice pink.

Mrs. Harlech Jones, Harlech View.

Fresh buttermilk used in the same way as cream with stewed fruit is most delicious and more economical.

Mrs. Clifford Evans, Manafon, Pentrefelin.

Angel Pudding.

2 oz butter, 2 oz sugar, 2 oz flour, 2 eggs, 1 gill milk. Beat butter to a cream, then beat in the sugar and yolks of eggs. Add flour, then milk very gradually, beating all just before baking. Time about 20 minutes. You can make it as a steamed pudding.

Miss Margaret Jones, Ty Newydd, Rhoslan.

Water Pudding.

12 tablespoonfuls of water, 2 tablespoonfuls of flour ¼ lb of butter. Boil these three ingredients together, stirring well, then add 5 eggs well beaten, yolks and whites separately, 1 lemon, rind and juice, add ½ lb of sugar. Mix all together and pour into a buttered dish. Bake half and hour, and serve at once. This can also be left to cool, turn out and cover with whipped cream.

Mrs. Griffiths, Talarfor.

Similar to the old 'hasty' pudding, using water instead of milk. A pudding like this was quickly made from the usual contents of the larder, hence its name. The result was much better than the name suggests.

Maynard Pudding.

6 oz sugar, 1 pint water, juice of one lemon, 2 tablespoonfuls cornflour (small ones) 2 eggs. Boil water and sugar. When boiling add cornflour, after it has been mixed with a little water. Boil for 10 minutes, add lemon juice, when cool add white of eggs beaten to a stifffroth. Make a custard with yolks, and serve round the mould.

Miss Moss, Caellobrith Lodge.

Cream Horns.

Roll puff paste out in lengths of one inch wide, twist round a tin, bake 15 minutes top shelf of a hot oven, but one minute before done gloss over with egg wash. When cold put a little raspberry jam, and fill up with whipped cream.

Mrs. Harlech Jones, Harlech View.

Orange Pudding.

Peel and cut four or five oranges into thin slices, removing all skin possible and pips. Lay the slices evenly in a dish. Sift over them a teacupful of castor sugar. Heat a pint of milk by letting it stand in boiling water, add the yolks of three eggs and tablespoonful of cornflour. Stir over fire until thick and then pour over the fruit. Beat the whites of the eggs to a stiff meringue with castor sugar, pile on the top of the pudding and put into the oven to harden and colour. Can be eaten either hot or cold. Enough for six people.

Mrs. Draper, Tan Lon.

Economical Pancake.

To 1 lb flour, 1 teaspoonful carbonate of soda, a pinch of salt. Make with sour milk into not too thin a batter, and fry in lard or any nice fat.

Mrs. Thomas, Gwalia.

Mont Blanc a la Marie-Reine.

Put about 18 or 20 chestnuts, peeled of the top skin, into the oven till the 2nd skin can be taken off. Put them in a little water in a saucepan with 8 or so lumps of sugar and a piece of lemon rind, and let them simmer till quite dry, tossing them occasionally so that they do not burn. Rub (not mash) them through a large-holed sieve, so that they come out grainy. Pile on a dish and surround with either whipped cream or whipped white of egg, flavoured with vanilla.

Mrs. Draper, Tan Lon.

A simple version of 'Mont Blanc aux Marrons', in which the chestnut 'vermicelli' surrounds a dome-shaped mound of Chantilly Cream.

SAVOURIES.

Cauliflower Cheese.

Break a cauliflower into pieces and boil. Take a breakfastcupful of breadcrumbs, the same of grated cheese, add a small piece of margarine, small teaspoonful of mustard, a little pepper and salt, nearly a pint of milk. Bring all to the boil, or until the cheese is all melted. Drain the cauliflower, place in a dish, and pour the sauce over it. Bake brown and serve very hot.

Miss Evans, Henfaes.

Savoury Cauliflower.

1 cauliflower, 1 oz butter, 1 oz flour, ½ pint milk, 2 oz grated cheese, pepper and salt. Wash and trim cauliflower. Put it into boiling water head downwards, boil very gently about 20 minutes. Take out carefully, drain on a sieve. Press gently with a cloth, put into a fire proof dish, (if possible) coat with sauce, and sprinkle over with cheese. Put into hot oven for a few minutes to brown.

Cheese Sauce.

Melt butter in a saucepan, stir in flour, add milk by degrees. Stir till it boils, and thickens. Add seasoning and half the cheese. Keep other half to put over cauliflower.

Mrs. Goodwill, Station House.

A dainty way of serving Macaroni.

Break enough long rows of macaroni to fill a breakfast cup. Throw it into a saucepan of boiling water, add a teaspoonful of salt and boil for 20 minutes. Pour off water, put in a piece of butter and two tablespoonfuls of grated cheese. Stir and keep hot whilst a few eggs are being poached. Have ready some nicely boiled green peas and when the eggs and macaroni are dished surround them with the green peas and serve immediately.

Miss Jones, Caerwylan.

Welsh Rarebit.

2 oz of cheese, 1 egg, 2 tablespoonful milk, a salt spoonful of mustard. Have ready some slices of toast, put grated cheese into a pan, break the egg, add the milk and mustard, let all come to the boil, pour over the toast, cut into neat pieces.

Miss Sinah Hughes, Bron Eifion.

Welsh Rarebit.

Ingredients: ½ lb of Cheshire or Cheddar Cheese, 1 oz butter, 2 tablespoonful of milk, 1 tablespoonful of made mustard, hot buttered toast. Method: Melt the butter in a stewpan, add the cheese cut in small pieces, stir until melted, then add the milk gradually, mustard and seasoning to taste. Have ready some hot buttered toast pour the cheese preparation on to it and serve as hot as possible.

Mrs. Thomas, Cardigan House.

Savoury Eggs.

Ingredients: ½ lb sausage meat, 3 or 4 hard boiled eggs, raw egg and breadcrumbs for coating. Method: boil three or four eggs for fifteen to 20 minutes and place them in a basin of cold water, peel the shell, wet the board well, shred out the sausage meat, having removed the skin. Take an egg and spread over the sausage meat, dip in raw egg, and brush it over, toss it well in the breadcrumbs. Fry separately in hot fat.

Miss Nan Williams, The Eifion.

Buttered Crab or Lobster.

Pull into light flakes with a couple of forks the flesh of the fish, put into a saucepan with a few bits of butter lightly rolled in flour, and heat slowly over the fire which must not be too quick. Then pour over and mix with from one to two tablespoonfuls of vinegar and a little cayenne pepper to taste. When the whole is well seasoned, stir constantly till thoroughly heated and then serve immediately either in it own shell or in scallop shells.

Mrs. Travers, Emu.

Comment: An old way with lobster or crab, and one of the best. Elize Acton included it in 'Modern Cookery for Private Families', pub. 1845.

Dainty Dish for High Tea.

Take six hard boiled eggs, cut them in half, take out the yolks, preserving the white entirely. Mix the yolks with a tablespoonful of anchovy and 1 oz of margarine, pepper to taste. Fill the whites with the mixture and serve on toast.

Miss Evans, Henfaes.

Macaroni Cheese.

2 oz macaroni, ½ pint milk, 1 oz flour, 1 oz butter, 3 oz grated cheese, pepper and salt to taste. Put macaroni in fast boiling water, pinch of salt, stir and then let it boil for about 20 minutes until quite soft. Strain it and cut into convenient pieces. Put the butter into the saucepan, and when melted stir in the flour and then add the milk by degrees, stirring all the time till it thickens and boils. Take off fire, bring to board, stir in the macaroni and cheese, keeping back a tablespoonful of cheese. Season again if necessary and put the mixture in a pie dish

Mrs. Goodwill, Station House.

Curried Cheese.

Fry in 1 oz of dripping or lard, a small onion and an apple well minced. When browned stir in one tablespoonful of flour and one small teaspoonful of curry powder made into a cream with milk. Simmer gently for a few minutes, then add 2 oz of grated cheese. Stir until well mixed and pour over rounds of well buttered toast. This is delicious for breakfast or supper.

Miss S. Roberts, Coedmor, Pentrefelin.

Cheese Finger.

Equal portions of flour, butter and grated cheese, no liquid. Roll out into a thin paste, cut out according to taste. Bake in a slow oven.

Mrs. Owen, Llety.

Yorkshire Pudding with Cheese.

1 lb flour, 6 oz cheese, 1 pint milk, 1 pint water.

Miss Moss, Caellobrith Lodge.

Potato Cheese.

1 ½ cooked potatoes, 3 oz grated cheese, 3 oz margarine, ½ pint milk, 1 egg, salt and pepper to taste. Mash potatoes, add margarine and ½ the cheese, mix thoroughly together with the beaten yolk of egg, whip white off egg to a stiff froth and stir in lightly. Put in greased pie dish and sprinkle with the remainder of cheese. This dish requires very little cooking, just enough to brown on the top.

Mrs. William George, Garth Celyn.

Cheese Pudding.

½ lb grated cheese, 2 eggs well beaten, 2 tablespoonfuls cream, ½ oz clarified butter. Beat all together, put in a buttered dish, and bake for ten minutes.

Mrs. Travers, Emu.

A nice Savoury.

A teacupful of sliced cheese, the same quantity of milk, 1 egg beaten, butter. Put the cheese in a pie dish, pour the milk over, then stir in the beaten egg. Bake 20 minutes.

Miss Myra Morgan, Bron Eifion.

Potted Savoury.

2 oz ham, 2 oz tongue, 3 oz Findon Haddock, 2 oz kippered herrings, 2 oz bloater, a few anchovies, lump of butter the size of an egg, anchovy sauce. Free from bones and pound in a mortar, put through a hair sieve and mix into a fine paste with anchovy sauce. (Red herring and hard roes can also be added). Put into a small jars and cover with melted butter. Keeps a long time.

Mrs. Benwell, Castle House.

Eggs a la Tripe.

Boil hard as many eggs as you want, cut in thick slices, keep two yolks and chop them up to garnish top. Lay eggs on a dish, make a good white sauce with yolk of egg and garnish round with sippets of toast.

Lady Ellis Nanney, Gwynfryn.

Savoury Pudding.

The night previous cut three or four slices of bread about ½ inch thick, pour over them boiling milk sufficient to cover them. In the morning bruise them and add 2 chopped onions partly boiled and a little suet, thyme and marjoram, 2 eggs, pepper and salt. Bake for half hour.

Mrs. Owen, Llys Caradog.

Scotch Woodcock.

Spread some essence of Anchovy on Toast, buttered and cut in pieces, according to taste. Beat up the yolks of one or two eggs, melt a little butter in good cream, then thicken it to the consistency of a good custard. Pour it over the buttered toast and anchovy and serve to table. N.B. - Care must be taken not to leave the yolk and cream too long on the fire or it will curdle.

Miss Priestly, Trefan.

Indian Kedgeree.

Wash ½ lb rice, 2 tablespoonfuls of lentils, and put in a saucepan with boiling water, salt and a few peppercorns, a few cloves, and a small piece of cinnamon stick, and boil for ¼ of an hour. Strain into a colander and dry. Put back into a saucepan with a piece of butter, shake together. Fry a sliced onion in butter or dripping. Also have ready a hard boiled egg. Place rice and lentils in a dish, place onion round it on top, also the egg cut in quarter. Garnish with parsley.

Mrs. Lewis, Llanystumdwy Rectory.

Onion Kedgeree.

Cut 4 or 5 large onions into square dice and fry for about 25 minutes over a moderate fire a slowly as you can, with seasoning of salt and pepper, being careful not to let them colour. Add a gill new milk, stir till boiling then gently simmer till the onions are tender and dry, when you add 4 oz plainly boiled rice and 6 hard boiled sliced eggs. Meanwhile in another pan put ½ oz creme de riz rubbed smooth with one gill each milk and cream, stir together till boiling, then pour this to the other ingredients, re-boil, turn out on hot dish, serve garnished with croutons.

Mrs. Drage, Parciau.

REAL OLD WELSH RECIPES.

Brwas.

Rhoddwch ychydig o fara ceirch o flaen y tân, er mwyn ei wneud yn crisp, ac yna ei falu hefo rhol bren heb fod yn rhy fân. Malwch llond cwpan de o fara gwyn, ac yna, ei roddi mewn bowlen ac ychydig bupur a halen, a llond llwy o dripping beef da (neu ragor os yn dewis), yna tywalltwch ddwfr berwedig arno a'i adael am ychydig funudau heb roddi bara ceirch ynddo. Yna rhoddwch y bara ceirch yn ysgafn, a gofalu nad oes gormod yn cael ei roddi i'w wneud yn rhy galed.

(Crumble a teacupful of white bread, put it in a basin, add a little salt, one teaspoonful of good dripping. Cover it with boiling water, let it remain for a few minutes, then crumble a little crisp oatmeal cake, and add it lightly on the top of it, not too much to make it hard).

Sican Gwyn.

Rhoddwch bowliad o flawd ceirch yn wlych mewn chwart o ddwfr oer, a hanner llond cwpan o laeth enwyn i'w suro, a'i adael yn wlych am ddwy noson. Yna tywalltwch y dwfr yn lan oddi arno, a chodi dwy lond llwyfwrdd o'r tywchedd a'i roddi drwy hidl, rhoddwch ato beint o ddwfr oer. Yna rhoddwch mewn sospan ac ychydig sinsir a siwgr fel yn dewis a'i ferwi am ddeng munud. Gellir rhoddi ychydig triog os yn dewis. Gellir cadw a gweddill o'r tywychedd am wythnos ond rhoddi dwfr ffres bob tro y cymerer peth ymaith.

(Cover a basinful of oatmeal with one quart of cold water and a half a teacupful of buttermilk, leave it to steep for two nights, then pour off the water. Put the thick portion through a sieve, adding another pint of cold water to it. Put it in a pan with a little ginger and sugar to taste. Boil for ten minutes stirring it all the time) .

Torth Gri.

Dwy lond powlen o flawd gwyn, 2 lond llwy o bowdwr crasu, 1 llond llwy de o egg powder, 2 lond llwy fwrdd o siwgr, ychydig halen, ¼ pwys o fenyn, ¼ pwys margarîn. Rhoddi'r powdwr crasu yn y blawd a rhwbio'r menyn a'r margarine ynddo a'i gymysgu hefo dwfr neu lefrith nes y byddo yn galed, yn cym-

38

ryd ychydig a'i rolio allan a'i roddi ar badell ar dân gweddol boeth.

(Two basinfuls of white flour, 2 teaspoonfuls of baking powder, 1 teaspoonful egg powder, 2 tablespoonfuls of sugar, pinch of salt, ¼ lb butter or margarine. Put baking powder and the egg powder in the flour, also rub in the butter, then mix altogether with a little milk, roll out and bake on a griddle).

Llymru.

Tair bowliad o flawd ceirch, 3 chwart o ddwfr am ei ben, 2 lond cwpan de o laeth enwin i'w suro. Adael yn wlych am ddwy noson, yna tywallt y dwfr i ffwrdd. Rhoddi chwart o ddwfr ffres at a'i hidlo trwy ogor. Roddir mewn sospan, a phan byddo yn dechrau berwi rhoddir dwy lond lwy fwrdd o beilliad wedi ei gymysgu yn dda hefo dwfr gan ei droi bob munud o'r adeg y bydd y saucepan yn cael ei rhoddi ar y tân. Gadael iddo ferwi am ddeng munud i chwarter awr ar dân cyflym a'i dywallt i lestr wedi ei wlychu a dwfr oer.

(Three basinfuls of oatmeal, 3 quarts of water, 2 teacupfuls of buttermilk. Cover the oatmeal with the water and buttermilk, let it remain for two nights, then pour off the water, add a little fresh water to it and put it through a sieve. Then put it in a pan, and when it begins to boil, add two tablespoonfuls of white flour to it, mixed with cold water and free from lumps. Boil all together for ten minutes, stir all the time).

Mrs. Jones, Glyn.

Llymru.

(A Welsh summer dish)

2 lbs oatmeal, buttermilk and water. Mix oatmeal with sufficient buttermilk and water to make a liquid consistency. Leave for two nights. Afterwards rinse through a hair sieve, let it stand and pour off the surface water. Simmer in a brass or enamel saucepan for 40 minutes and keep stirring. Serve with sweet milk and salt

Mrs. Morris, Ty Cerrig.

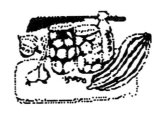

PICKLES

Catwad Maro/Marrow Chutney

Malwch chwe pwys o maro fel siwgwr gwyn rhowch mewn sospan gyda tri hanner peint o finigr, malwch 1 pwys o falau yn fân, 1 pwys o wnionyn, ¼ pwys o halen, 1 pwys o siwgwr a gadewch iddynt ferwi nes bydd y maro yn ddigon, yna rhoddwch 1 owns o sinsir mâl, 1 owns powdwr tiwmerig, a hanner tin o fwstard wedi ei gymysgu hefo finigr oer a'i adael i ferwi am bum munud wedyn.

(Cut up 6 lbs of marrow into small chunks like loaf sugar place in a saucepan with 1 ½ pint vinegar, cut up 1 lb apples, and 1 lb onions, ¼ lb of salt, 1 lb of sugar, and let this all boil with the marrow until it is tender. Then add 1 oz ground giner, 1 oz turmeric, and half a small tin of mustard, mixed with cold vinegar, and boil all up for 5 minutes.

Mrs. E. Jones, Highgate, Llanystumdwy.

Catwad Maro/Marrow Chutney

Malwch chwe pwys o maro fel siwgwr gwyn, rhowch mewn sospan gyda tri hanner peint o finigr malwch 1 pwys o falau yn fân, 1 pwys o wnionyn, ¼ pwys o halen, 1 pwys o siwgwr a gadewch iddynt ferwi nes bydd y maro yn ddigon, yna rhoddwch 1 owns o sinsir mâl, 1 owns powdwr tiwmerig, a hanner tin o fwstard wedi ei gymysgu hefo finigr oer a'i adael i ferwi am bum munud wedyn.

(Cut up 6 lbs of marrow into small chunks like loaf sugar place in a saucepan with 1 ½ pint vinegar, cut up 1 lb apples, and 1 lb onions, ¼ lb of salt, 1 lb of sugar, and let this all boil with the marrow until it is tender. Then add 1 oz ground giner, 1 oz turmeric, and half a small tin of mustard, mixed with cold vinegar, and boil all up for 5 minutes.

Mrs. E. Jones, Highgate, Llanystumdwy.

Marrow Chutney.

1 marrow, 1 quart vinegar, 1 lb apples, ½ lb onions, ½ oz ground giner, ½ oz cayenne and mustard, 2 oz loaf sugar, ½ turmeric powder. Cut marrow, sprinkle with salt, boil ingredients for 15 minutes, mix turmeric powder with the mustard before adding.

Mrs. E. Jones, Highgate, Llanystumdwy.

Chutney.

2 lbs vegetable marrow, ½ lb shallots or any onion cut small, 1 ½ pints vinegar, 1 lb cooking apples, ½ Ib sugar, a few chillies, ½ oz bruised ginger. Peel and cut the marrow in rather small chunks, sprinkle with salt and let it stand for 12 hours. Then strain and add above ingredients, putting all in a pan and boil for ½ hour. The spices to be put in a muslin bag. After boiling all ingredients for ½ hour mix 1 oz turmeric powder with a tablespoonful of cornflour with a little vinegar into a smooth paste and boil again for three or four minutes stirring all the time.

Mrs. W. H. Williams, Manchester House.

Green Tomato Chutney.

2 lbs each of tomatoes, apples and onions, cook together in their own juice in a covered pan. Add ½ teaspoonful cayenne pepper, a few peppercorns, salt to taste, and about 1 pint vinegar until of required thickness. Boil up and bottle while hot.

Mrs. Bartleman, Ymwlch.

Pickled Damsons.
(Cheshire Recipe)

Pick 4 quarts of damsons, pour over them a quart of white wine vinegar, and let them stand all night. Then pour off the syrup, adding to it 4 lbs of sugar and boil for 20 minutes. Pour it over the damsons and again let it stand all night. Next day pour off the syrup and boil ½ hour with cloves tied up in a muslin bag. Put the damson into jars or bottles and pour syrup over them.

Mrs. Owen, Llety.

Salad Dressing.

1 egg, ½ pint milk, tablespoonful sugar, mustard, a little salt. Enough vinegar to thicken it.

Mrs. Owen, Llys Caradog.

Salad Dressing.

Boil together one teaspoonful of butter, 1 teaspoonful of flour and teacupful of milk. Then add to the mixture 1 cup of vinegar, 2 tablespoonful of sugar, 2 eggs, 1 teaspoonful of salt, 2 teaspoonful of mustard. Stir well together until it thickens but do not let it boil, if it is too thick add a little more milk. This keeps some time, bottled and well corked.

Mrs. Cybi Jones, Bryntirion Terrace.

Pickled Pears.

(small hard Pears)

To every 30 pears use ¾ lb sugar and one pint of vinegar. A few red peppers. Peel and halve the pears and stick three or four cloves in each half. Boil in the vinegar and sugar until tender. Try it with a fork and when tender take out and place in jars. Pour the vinegar over when cool and cover.

Mrs. G.P. Williams, The Eifion.

Home Made Mixed Pickles.

Ingredients: Shallots, cauliflower, french beans, scarlet runners, cucumbers and marrow. Method: Cut up all the vegetables into small chunks, put onions and cauliflower to stand in salt and water over night. Next day put all vegetables in a pan, and sprinkle with salt and 1 oz turmeric powder, and pour on a quart of vinegar and bring to the boil. Have ready mixed 6 oz mustard with a little cold vinegar, and mix well. Then it is ready for bottling, do not put vinegar in mixture after adding mustard.

Miss M.A. Evans, Rhianfa.

Tomato Chutney.

For each 2 lbs of tomatoes take 1/2 lb sugar and the same of apples, 2 oz salt, ½ oz mustard seed, 1 oz ginger, 3 or 4 small onions, a grain or two of cayenne pepper, and a little over ½ pint of malt vinegar. Break the tomatoes, quarter the apples, chop the onions and crush the mustard seed. Place all in a pan (except the sugar) and simmer gently until soft enough to be rubbed through and sieve. When the vinegar is hot, add the sugar and stir well. After the chutney has been well pulped place it in an earthenware jar for at least 24 hours before bottling.

Miss Gladys Roe, High Street.

Chutney.

2 soup plates of sour apples sliced, ½ lb dried apricots soaked in 1 quart of vinegar till soft, 5 large onions, 1 garlic, half soup- plateful red chillies, 1 lb

sugar, 1 large breakfastcupful of stoned raisins, ½ lb green tomatoes, ½ lb salt, ½ lb ginger, 1 tablespoonful of mustard seed. All these ingredients to be bruised fine. The garlic and onions minced. The raisins stoned, the other ingredients to be well mixed. The whole to be boiled in three quarts of vinegar till it looks clear.

Mrs. Williams, Ynysgain

Walnuts Pickled.

Ingredients: Green walnuts. To 3 pints of vinegar, allow 1 oz of salt and ½ oz each of all spices, peppercorns, cloves and whole ginger. Method: wipe the walnuts with a dry cloth, prick them with a steel fork or a large darning needle, put them in widenecked bottles or unglazed jars and cover them with cold vinegar. Cover closely, let them stand in a cold dry place for 4 months, then drain off the vinegar. Boil as much fresh vinegar as will cover them, with the seasonings stated above, pour it while boiling hot over the walnuts. Cover closely and store for three weeks in a cool place. The walnuts will then be ready for use.

Mrs. Thomas, Cardigan House.

SCONES AND CAKES.

Scones.

1 lb flour, 3 oz lard, 1 teaspoonful cream of tartar, 1 teaspoonful carbonate of soda, a little sugar. Mix with new milk and bake for twenty minutes.

Mrs. W. H. Williams, Manchester House.

Scotch Scones.

Basin of flour, little teaspoonful of salt, teaspoonful carbonate soda, sugar to taste. Mix with buttermilk to a batter, fry in lard in a frying pan or on a griddle to a light brown, and butter when hot or cold.

Mrs. J.W. Thomas, Parciau Ucha.

43

Whole Meal Scones.

4 teacupfuls of flour 1 ½ teacupfuls whole meal, 5 oz margarine, ½ teacupful of sugar, a small teaspoonful of salt mixed with the sugar, a small teaspoonful of carbonate of soda, a small teaspoonful cream of tartar. Make into a dough with sweet milk, cut into squares and bake in a moderate oven.

Mrs. McKerrow, Blecarlo.

Barley Scones.

Ingredients: ½ lb self-raising flour, 1 breakfastcupful barley flour, half teaspoonful carbonate of soda, ¼ teaspoonful of tartar, pinch of salt, 1 egg (or egg substitute), ¼ lb lard, 2 oz sugar, buttermilk to rise if egg is not sufficient. Method: Cream the sugar and lard, then beat the egg well and add to the cream, then miz all the flour etc. together and add by degrees to it till all is well mixed. If a stiff dough is obtained no buttermilk will be required. Cut in rounds and lay on a greased tin. Bake in quick oven for 14 minutes.

Mrs. K.G. Roberts, Plymouth.

Buttermilk Scones.

Mix thoroughly into a bowl 8 tablespoonfuls of flour, a dessertspoonful of castor sugar, half a teaspoonful of carbonate of soda, the same of cream of tartar, and a pinch of salt. Rub in a piece of margarine about the size of an egg. Add a few currants and mix with buttermilk into a stiff dough. Cut into small scones and bake in a brisk oven.

Mrs. Brooks, Wern Ddu.

Scones.

1 lb flour, 2 oz margarine or lard, 1 teaspoonful of carbonate soda, half teaspoonful cream of tartar, 1 teaspoonful sugar, 1 oz current, about half pint buttermilk. The butter or margarine to be well rubbed into the flour, add all dry ingredients, and thoroughly mix them, then mix with buttermilk. Roll it out on a board, about 1 inch thick. Cut either into triangular shapes, or use a cutter to make into round cakes. Bake in a hot oven about half an hour.

Mrs. Ebenezer Thomas, Mynydd Ednyfed.

Tea Cake.

¼ lb flour, 2 oz castor sugar, 2 oz butter, 1 egg, 1 heaped teaspoonful of baking powder, very little buttermilk. Rub butter into flour, beat well into a smooth paste and bake for 20 minutes, to be eaten hot.

Mrs. W. H. Williams, Manchester House.

Welsh Gridle Cakes.

1 lb of flour, 6 oz butter or margarine, 6 oz sugar, pinch of salt, 2 oz currants, half teaspoonful carbonate of soda and buttermilk to mix. Mix well flour, salt, sugar and butter, then add currants and carbonate of soda. Break in the egg and mix with buttermilk. Turn out on a floured board and roll out into small cakes about ¼ inch thickness, and bake both sides on a hot gridle or frying pan.

Mrs. Morris, Ty Cerrig.

Potato Cake.

Cold mashed potatoes. Mix with a little flour, melt a little lard, sugar and a little carbonate of soda, mix all with milk into a firm dough. Can be baked in an oven or on a frying pan.

Mrs. J.W. Thomas,- Parcia Ucha.

Potato Cake.

2 cupfuls of flour, 1 teaspoonful of salt, 1 teaspoonful of baking powder, 1 tablespoonful of lard or dripping, three small potatoes mixed with the ingredients before adding sweet or sour milk. Make a medium stiff paste. Form a generous sized biscuit and bake.

Mrs. Griffiths, Talafor.

Fadge.
(an Irish Breakfast or Tea Bread)

2 cupfuls of flour, 1 teaspoonful of salt, 1 teaspoonful of baking powder, 1 tablespoonful of lard or dripping, three small potatoes mixed with the ingredients before adding sweet or sour milk. Make a medium stiff paste. Form a generous sized biscuit and bake.

Mrs. Griffiths, Talafor.

Tasty Breakfast Dish.

4 tablespoonfuls of flour, half teaspoonful of baking powder, a pinch of salt, enough sour milk to mix in a batter. Mix the flour and salt with the milk, adding the baking powder just before you begin to cook it. Then fry a nice brown in the fat after the bacon.

Mrs. Jones, Caellobrith Terrace.

Welsh Crempog (Pancakes), a device to "stretch" the supply of breakfast bacon when time were hard.

45

Plain Shortbread.

Take ½ lb of slightly powdered butter rub it with the hands into one lb of flour and 4 oz crushed loaf sugar. Making it into a smooth ball, and roll out in two round cakes about ¾ inch thick. Prick it over with a fork, pinch round the edges, and bake in a moderate oven for half an hour.

Mrs. Jones, Caellobrith Terrace.

Shortbread.

¼ lb butter, 2 oz castor sugar, ¼ lb flour 2 oz ground rice. Instead of ground rice you can use cornflour Cream the butter and sugar together, until they are quite whilc. To economise the butter, you can use half lard and half butter. Put the flour and ground rice together through the sieve. Take a knife and add them by degrees to the butter. Do not use your hand to put in the flour and ground rice as it will clot the butter. If your like all flour can be used, but the ground rice will make it more crisp. Mix well with a spoon, put all the flour in, then mix with your hand, you want to knead it as much as you would knead bread. You must remember that in Shortbread you do not want any water to mix, the butter is enough. After getting it into a smooth ball, turn it out on the board lightly floured, roll out about half an inch thick. Shortbread must not be too thin. Keep it quite smooth without cracking, ornament the edges, put it in the oven to bake until it is a light brown, and be careful that it does not break in lifting it on to the tin.

Miss E.C. Jones, Parkia Ucha.

Orange Cake.

6 oz sugar, 4 oz flour, 2 oranges, 2 eggs, 2 teaspoonfuls baking powder. Beat the eggs and sugar for ten minutes, add the juice of 1½ orange and rind of one orange, and the flour and baking powder. Put into two tins and bake in a moderate oven for 20 minutes. Put the juice of the half orange mixed with sugar between the two cakes after baking.

Miss A. Jones, Henlyn.

Tea Cakes.

1 bowl flour, ¼ lb butter, ¼ lb sugar, 3 eggs, 1 tablespoonful of carbonate of soda, 2 tablespoonful of cream of tartar, 1 tablespoonful of cream of tartar, 1 tablespoonful of baking powder. Mix with buttermilk, bake in a moderate hot oven.

Mrs. Humphreys, Aberkin.

Cake.

1 cup of butter, 2 cups of sugar, 2 cups of flour, one and a half cups sultanas, ½ cup milk, a little salt, 2 eggs, mixed peel, 1½ tablespoonfuls baking powder. Mix butter and sugar, beat up eggs, white and yolks, separately. Put in the yolks, then the flour and sultanas. Mix all together and bake for ¾ hours.

Miss S. Roberts, Coedmor, Pentrefelin.

Delicious Cake.

¼ lb butter, ½ lb flour, 4 oz castor sugar, 2 eggs, about ½ cupful of milk, teaspoonful of baking powder. Beat sugar and butter to a cream, add the yolks of 2 eggs and flour alternately and milk, add the baking powder and the whites of eggs well beaten. Mix well. Bake in a moderate oven.

Miss Hughes, Trefan.

Swiss Cakes.

Cream 6 oz butter with 3 oz sugar, add one egg, and beat well, sift in 7 oz flour and 1 teaspoonful baking powder. Bake in patty pans for about 15 minutes.

Mrs. Davies, Bron Eifion Lodge.

Gingerbread.

1½ lbs flour, 6 oz lard, butter or margarine, 6 oz sugar, ¾ lb treacle, 2 teaspoonful carbonate of soda, half ounce ground ginger, a little milk or buttermilk, rub the butter into the flour, add the dry ingredients, mix to a stiff batter with the treacle and milk. Put into a greased tin and bake in a slow oven for 1 hour.

Miss Marian P. Williams, The Eifion.

Very Good Gingerbread.

¾ lb flour, ¾ lb black treacle, 3 oz margarine, ¾ oz ground ginger, ¾ teaspoonful carbonate soda, 2 eggs, milk to mix, a pinch of salt. Weigh a basin, and weigh the treacle into it, so as not to lose any. Rub the fat into flour, and add the soda, sugar and ginger, stir these into the treacle and then add well beaten eggs. Make into a soft dough with a little milk, and place in a flat greased tin in quick oven. When done turn out on sieve and cut up with a hot knife at once and then let cool. Candied peel in the dough, and a few shredded blanched almond the top add to the goodness of this gingerbread, but it is excellent without.

Mrs. Draper, Tan Lôn.

Parkyn.

1 lb oatmeal, 1 lb flour, 6 oz dripping or lard, ½ teaspoon mixed spice, ½ teaspoon ground ginger, 12 oz golden syrup, 2 teaspoonful baking powder. Melt the syrup dripping or lard. Mix the dry ingredients, adding a small cupful of milk. Bake in a flat tin for two hours in a slow oven.

Mrs. Pritchard, Sheffield House.

Ginger Cake.

1 lb flour, 6 oz butter or margarine, 6 oz fine sugar, 3 eggs, 1 teacupful of syrup, 1 teacupful of milk, 1 teaspoonful of carbonate of soda, 1 teaspoonful ground ginger, 1 teaspoonful all spice. A pinch of salt. Cream butter and sugar, then drop in yolks or eggs and beat well. Add syrup, soda and seasonings milk and lastly flour. Then the whites of eggs beaten to a stiff froth. Mix well and put in a tine lined with greased paper. Bake in a moderate oven for 1 1/2 to 2 hours.

Mrs. W. Talmage Davies, Llys Owen.

Sponge Cake.

2 eggs, their weight in sugar and flour, 2 teaspoons baking powder. Cream the sugar and butter together, break in the two eggs, beat to a light batter. Add the flour lightly through a sieve, "gogor", mix with a fork, add a little milk if too stiff. Put in a greased tin and bake in hot oven for 20 minutes.

Miss Maggies Jones, 1 Pensingrig.

Sponge Cake.

2 eggs, ¼ lb flour, ¼ lb sugar, ½ teaspoonful baking powder. Beat the eggs and sugar thoroughly well, add the flour and baking powder. Bake about ½ hour.

Mrs. Janet Jones, 2 Pensingrig.

Lemon Biscuits.

½ lb flour, ½ teaspoonful baking powder, 2 oz sugar, 2 oz butter, half a rind of lemon, yolk of an egg. Grate the lemon rind in the flour, knead altogether and roll out. Cut with a round cutter, and bake a golden brown.

Miss Roberts, Gwynfryn Lodge.

Seed Cake.

1 lb flour, 2 teaspoonfuls baking powder, 5 oz brown or castor sugar, ½ oz caraway seeds, 8 oz dripping or butter, one or two eggs. Beat a little water up with the eggs. Mix very dry, and bake 1½ hours.

Miss Margaret Tones. Ty Newvdd, Rhoslan.

Plain Buns.

Take 8 oz flour, 3 oz margarine, 3 oz sugar, 3 oz sultanas, 1 oz lemon peel, 1 teaspoonful baking powder. Beat up margarine and sugar, then mix all together. Cut into small portions, place on tin and bake until done.

Mrs. E. Jones, Highgate, Llanystumdwy.

Plain Cake without Eggs.

1 lb flour, 8 oz sugar, 4 oz currants, 8 oz raisins, ¼ pint milk (a little more if needed), 6 oz lard or margarine, 1 tablespoonful of black treacle, half teaspoonful salt, 1 teaspoonful carbonate of soda, a small wine glass of vinegar. Rub the lard or butter into the flour, add the sugar, currants, and stoned raisins. Dissolve the soda in a little milk and then mix all together, adding the vinegar the last of all. Pour into a tine lined with greased paper and bake in rather a slow oven.

Mrs. Hugh Williams, Pentrefelin Vicarage.

Currant Cake.

8 oz flour, 4 oz each sugar and currants, 1 large teaspoonful baking powder, pinch of salt, 2 eggs, 3 oz butter, half teacup milk. Mix flour, salt, baking powder, rub in the butter, add sugar and cleaned currants. Make into a stiff paste with beaten egg and milk. Bake in a flat tin or in a loaf.

Mrs. Lloyd Owen, Bank House.

Delicious Almond Cakes.

This is a good way of using up the trimmings of pastry when making a fruit tart. Also the yolks of eggs when whites are used for icing or sweet-making. Ingredients: Pastry, 2 oz ground almonds, 4 oz sugar, 5 drops of almond essence, 1 teaspoonful of lemon juice, 1 egg or the yolks of two eggs. Method: Line patty pans with thin pastry. Mix together the almonds, sugar essence, and add the well-whipped egg. Three parts fill the patty pans with the mixture, cross the tops with two narrow strips of pastry, and bake in a moderate oven.

Miss Margaret Jones, Ty Newydd, Rhoslan.

Cakes.

4 oz Quaker oats, 2 oz margarine, 2 oz sugar, a few drops of essence of almonds, or vanilla, mix all well together, and bake in patty pans. A little flour makes them bind better.

Miss Whitaker, Marine Crescent.

New Year's Bun.

2 lbs dough, work ¼ lb butter into it. Keep it warm 2 hours that i may rise. Meanwhile stone 2 lb raisins, clean 1 lb currants, cut 1 lb orange peel into strips, blanch and cut ½ lb Valencia almonds, and mix ½ oz ground ginger with 1 oz sweet spice. Cut off a fourth part of the dough for a cover, mix all the fruit and spice in what remains. When thoroughly mixed, butter your cake tin and press in the mixture to mould it. Roll out the remaining dough quite thin, brush it over with water, turn out the centre of the dough, cover it all over, cutting off any pieces that overlap, put again into the cake tin with smooth side uppermost. Brush over the beaten egg, and prick over with a fork, take a skewer, and pierce it here and there to the bottom of the pan. Bake in a moderate oven for two hours.

Mrs. McKerrow, Belcarlo.

Queen Cake.

1 lb flour, 8 oz butter, ¼ lb sugar, 1 oz peel, 2 oz almonds, 3 eggs, ¼ pint of milk. Beat the butter to a cream, whisk the eggs, whites and yolks separately, bleach and chop the almonds and cup up the peel. Mix together, add the milk then the flour and beat well for a few minutes. Bake for rather more than one and a half hours in a shallow tin.

Miss C.A. Rowlands, High Street.

Two Cakes Made Without Sugar.

King's Cake.

Ingredients: 10 oz flour, 5 oz margarine, 2 dried eggs, 1 gill milk, pinch of salt, 2 small tablespoonfuls of syrup, 1 teaspoonful baking powder, 8 oz sultanas. Method: Sieve the flour, salt and baking powder, rub in the margarine, clean the sultanas, and add. Mix the milk and syrup together, prepare the eggs according to the directions, beat well, add to the milk, and stir into the dry ingredients. Put into a greased tin, lined with greased paper, and bake in a moderate oven for one hour.

Queen's Cake.

Ingredients: 8 oz flour, 1 teaspoonful baking powder, 1 good tablespoonful of syrup, 1 oz of any kind of chopped nuts, 1 oz of sultanas, pinch of salt, 1 teaspoonful of powdered cinnamon, 3 oz of margarine, 1 teacupful of sour milk. Method: Sieve the salt, baking powder and flour, also the cinnamon. Rub in the margarine, clean the sultanas, blanch and chop the nuts, which should be weighed after chopping: add to the flour mixture. Beat well, then put the mixture into a greased cake tin, lined with greased paper, bake in a moderate oven one hour.

Mrs. Oldfield, Breeze Hill.

Simple Recipe for Simnel Cake.

8 oz of butter, 12 oz flour, 5 eggs, half teaspoonful each of mixed spice and baking powder, 1 lb ground almonds, 12 oz currants, 1 lb castor sugar, 4 oz candied peel, the juice of half a lemon. First make an almond paste by mixing together in a basin the almonds and half the sugar, then melt 2 oz of butter, separate the whites of 2 of the eggs, and whisk them stiff. Add these with the yolks to the almonds, and work into a paste. Roll out. Cream the butter and sugar, add the spice, and beat in the eggs one at a time. Stir in the flour by degrees, and lastly the fruit and baking powder. Grease a square tin, line it with greased paper, pour in half the cake mixture, and spread over it half the almond paste, the pour in the other half of the mixture. Bake in a good oven about 2 to 3 hours. When the cake is about three parts cooked arrange the other half of the almond paste in a roll round the top of it, and finish baking slowly.

Mrs. Gwen Jones, Lonsingrig.

Economical Sandwich

Cream together three large tablespoonfuls of castor or fine sugar, one good tablespoonful of margarine, break in one large egg again beat well. Add by degrees 4 tablespoonfuls of flour, if stiff add a little milk, and lastly half small teaspoonful of carbonate of soda, and ½ small teaspoonful cream of tartar. Beat well together. Bake in a hot oven for about 7 minutes on a flat tin lined with greased paper. When done turn out and spread one half with raspberry jam or lemon cheese, turning the other half over. Press neatly. When cold, if desired, can be cut into finger and decorated with dessicated coconut.

Miss S.A. Jones, Tyn Gate.

Economical Sandwich.

Cream together three large tablespoonfuls of castor or fine sugar, one good tablespoonful of margarine, break in one large egg, again beat well. Add by degrees 4 tablespoonfuls of flour, if stiff add a little milk, and lastly half small teaspoonful of carbonate of soda, and ½ small teaspoonful cream of tartar. Beat well together. Bake in a hot oven for about 7 minutes on a flat tin lined with greased paper. When done turn out and spread one half with raspberry jam or lemon cheese, turning the other half over. Press neatly. When cold, if desired, can be cut into finger and decorated with dessicated coconut.

Miss S.A. Jones, Tyn Gate.

Jam Sandwich without Eggs.

½ lb flour, 1 teaspoonful of baking powder, ¼ lb margarine, 2 ½ oz castor sugar. Mix the baking powder, and flour, cream the sugar and margarine, then mix in the flour, with 3 or 4 tablespoonfuls of milk, making a fairly stiff mixture. Well grease a sandwich tin and dust with flour. Put in the mixture and press down with the hand and smooth over with water. Bake in moderate oven for 20 minutes. When cool cut through and spread with jam

Mrs. Griffith, Railway Hotel.

Two Jam Sandwiches made with one Egg.

12 oz flour, 1 egg, 8 oz margarine, 2 teaspoonfuls baking powder. Buttermilk to mix. Warm margarine and add sugar and beat to a cream, beat in the egg, then the buttermilk, add flour and lastly the baking powder. Bake in two greased tins in a moderate oven. This takes rather a long time to bake.

Mrs. Rowlands, Bryntirion Terrace.

Currant Bread.

4 lbs flour, 3 lbs currants, 1 nutmeg, ½ lb candied peel, 1 lb 8 oz sugar, 1 oz cream of tartar, 1 oz carbonate soda, 1 pkt baking powder. Mix with buttermilk. This quantity makes several loaves.

Mrs. Rowlands, Bryntirion Terrace.

Bun Loaf.

2 lbs flour, 6 oz margarine, 6 oz lard, 8 oz brown sugar, 1 lb currants, 8 oz peel, 8 oz raisins, 2 oz barm. Rub margarine and lard well into the flour and mix sugar and fruit and knead into a soft dough with barm and allow about 2 hours to rise.

Mrs. Davies, Stanley Stores.

Date Cake.
(Canadian Recipe)

1 lb dates, ¼ lb butter or margarine, 1 teacup brown sugar, 1 teacup raisins, 1 teacup walnuts, 3 teacups flour, 1 tablespoon treacle, 2 eggs, ¾ cupful warm water, 1 teaspoonful carbonate soda. Mix ingredients with the melted butter, keeping the walnuts as whole as possible, melt carbonate soda in warm water. Bake about 1 hour in slow oven.

Mrs. William George, Garth Celyn.

JAMS.

Orange Marmalade.

Have a dozen Seville Oranges, slice them finely, removing all pips. To every lb of cut fruit, add three pints of water. After being cut let it stand in the water until next day. Then boil briskly half hour. The following day weigh it, and to every lb of the cut fruit add 1 lb loaf sugar, boil from one and half to two hours. If there is 10 lbs of fruit, 9 lbs of sugar will be sufficient.

Mrs. Thomas, Stable House, Bron Eifion.

Rhubarb and Fig Jam.

6 lbs rhubarb, 5 lbs sugar, 8 oz figs, candied peel. Cut figs and peel very fine, put over rhubarb with sugar over night. Boil one and half hour.

Miss Griffith, Brynderwen.

Marrow Jam.

Ingredients: Marrows, sugar, ginger. Method: Peel and slice the marrows and remove all the seeds. To every 1 lb of marrow allow ¾ lb sugar which must be placed in alternate layers with the shred marrow and allowed to remain undisturbed for not less than 12 hours. When ready boil gently for about an hour, then add a teaspoonfill of ginger, to each 4 lbs of marrow. Stir well until mixed, and turn into pots or glass jars, cover with parchment paper and store in a dry place.

Miss Griffith, Brynderwen.

53

Blackberry and Apple Cheese.

Take windfalls and small apples, wash, add half the amount in blackberries and put in preserving pan, cover with water and boil until apples are soft, then press through fine wire sieve until only pips and skins are left. To every ping of pulp allow 1 lb of sugar. Boil until it sets and pot while hot. This is a most economical jam for children.

Mrs. Evans Jones, Ymwlch.

Elderberry Jam.

Allow ¾ lb of sugar to every lb of fruit. Strip the fruit from the stalks, boil in very little water for 5 minutes. Add the sugar and lemon (tablespoonful) and boil for 45 minutes.

Mrs. Cambriensis Williams, Eryldon.

Green Gooseberry Jam.

1 quart water, 3 lbs of green gooseberries (not overgrown), 4 lbs 8 oz crystallised sugar. Boil the water and fruit together for 20 minutes, after coming to an all round boil, then add sugar and boil together after coming to boil all round. Have your jars hot, fill with fruit, cover and put away at once.

Mrs. Fowden Jones, Eisteddfa.

Tomato Jam.

To each lb of green tomatoes sliced add ¾ lb of sugar and one lemon. Boil for half an hour. The flavour is like greengage.

Mrs. Burnell, Parkia Terrace.

Two pleasant and very wholesome breakfast Jams.

Apple.

To 4 lbs apples, peeled, cut and cored, add 3 lbs sugar, 1 tablespoonful ordinary black treacle, the juice and grated rind of one small or half a large lemon.

Rhubarb.

To 6 lbs rhubarb, after the stringy outside has been peeled off, cut in squared, add 3 lbs sugar, a good tablespoonful of black treacle, the juice and grated rind of half a lemon and ¼ oz grated ginger. For each jam, put into saucepan and boil 2½ to 3 hours, to test when it is done, put a little in a saucer at the open window, and if on holding it up, the surface is seen to skim over, the jam is done. They keep two years or more.

Mrs. Greaves, Bron Eifion.

Apricot Jam.

2 lbs dried apricots, 5 pints water, 7 lbs loaf sugar. Cut up and cover the apricots with water for two days. Boil with sugar for half an hour, or until it sets. This should make four lbs of jam.

Miss Moss, Caellobrith Lodge.

Gooseberry Jelly.

A pint of water to six pints of gooseberries boil until soft enough to strain through a sieve, add 1 lb sugar to each pint of juice, boil until it jellies.

Mrs. J.W. Thomas, Parciau Ucha.

Rhubarb Jelly.

Cut the rhubarb into inch lengths, put them in an earthenware pan in a hot oven till the juice comes out, then put through a sieve overnight. Boil the juice quickly for 20 minutes and to every pint add 1¼ lb loaf sugar. Mind not to touch a spoon in it. Lemon juice can be added if desired.

Mrs. J.W. Thomas, Parciau Ucha.

Medlar Jelly.

Take medlars when quite ripe, wash them, and put them into a preserving pan with as much water as will cover them. Let them stew slowly till they become a pulp. Then put them through a jelly bag, and to every pint of liquid put ¾ lb of loaf sugar. Boil it quickly for half hour or until it jellies. It should be clear and bright in colour when done.

Miss Hughes, Trefan.

THINGS USEFUL TO KNOW.

Embrocation.

Half pint each of wine vinegar and spirits of turpentine, 2 oz each of camphor, laudanum, and cayenne pepper. The white of two eggs, beaten and added slowly.

Mrs. Thomas, Stable House, Bron Eifion.

To Remove Tar Stains from Clothes.

Scrape off as much as possible of the tar with a knife while it is soft. Then work a little butter into the tar, rubbing it in gently until the butter shows through on the other side. Wash off with soap and warm water.

Miss Allen, Parciau.

Fruit Salts.

¾ lb cream of tartar, ¾ lb carbonate of soda, ¾ lb tartaric acid, ½ lb castor sugar, 2 oz Epsom salts. Keep in a cool place and cork well. Dose 1 teaspoon in water.

The best Food for Bottle-fed Baby at six months old.

Soak a tablespoonful of oatmeal in a small basin of cold water all night. Next morning squeeze it through strong muslin. Put on a small saucepan to boil a little water, not quite a teacup; when boiling put in the strained oatmeal, and boil gently for an hour in a covered saucepan, not fast over a hot fire. Use it for baby's bottle instead of water and milk, once a day. Begin twice a week, then every day. Oatmeal is the best for building good bone, and flesh; and made according to this recipe will never disagree. Later on the child takes readily to porridge. Buy good country oatmeal ground at a neighbouring mill.

Mrs. Greaves, Bron Eifion.

Camphor Ice.

1 oz oil of almonds, ½ oz camphor, 1 oz spermaceti, ¼ oz white wax. Melt all together and place in pot. For chapped lips etc.

Mrs. Benwell, Castle House.

Ointment for Cuts and Wounds.

3d. worth each of Swallow oil, Eucalyptus oil, Vaseline, Beeswax, Camphor. Put all together in a jar in the oven to melt, then run into small tins with lids, and cover tight.

Miss Myra Morgan, Bron Eifion.

Home-made Barm.

½ oz hops, 2 large potatoes, not peeled, 2 teacupfuls of barley. Boil all these for half an hour. Then set aside till lukewarm. Add to it 1 teacupful of flour, 1/4 1b granulated sugar, a pinch of salt, and ½ oz of fresh yeast. Leave to ferment for 24 hours. Put the mixture through a fine sieve, and put into bottles. A teacupful of this barm will rise 4 lbs of flour. Always keep a little to start the fresh lot of barm instead of the yeast.

Mrs. Jones, Caellobrith Terrace.

To keep Fish fresh.

(West coast of Ireland Recipe).

Have ready a cauldron of boiling water and throw in a handful of common salt. Lift the fish instantly in and out, only for a second immerse them, and it "sets" them, as it is called.

Mrs. Hugh Williams, Pentrefelin Vicarage.

Patent Flour.

2 ½ lbs flour, 1 ¼ oz cream of tartar, ¾ oz carbonate of soda. Sift all together and keep in an airtight tin. The longer it is kept the better.

Mrs. Harlech Jones, Harlech View.

To bake Potatoes quickly.

Soak them for ten minutes in boiling water to which add a little salt, remove them and place in the oven, and they will take but a short time to bake.

Mrs. A. K. Hughes, Maenwern.

To prevent Jam from going mouldy.

Cut rounds of tissue paper size of jars, soak each in vinegar, separately, and lay close over the top of jam. Cover in the usual way. Proved and found successful.

Mrs. Clifford Evans, Minafon, Pentrefelin.

Virtues of Vinegar.

Two or three tablespoonfuls of vinegar will prove most refreshing to a tired individual, especially if one has been out walking in the heat.

A few drops of vinegar in a tumbler of water is a splendid mouth wash.

Vinegar in washing-up water cleanses grease, brightens and disinfects china.

Vinegar and salt remove ink stains from the fingers.

Vinegar and bath brick remove rust from flat irons.

A little vinegar added to water in which vegetables are steeped will make same fresh and crisp and will destroy insects.

Vinegar and salt will clean glass flower vases, water bottles, etc.

Vinegar added to blacklead will give a more lasting polish to the grate.

A teaspoonful of vinegar should be added to water when boiling fish or poaching eggs.

Vinegar and water, equal parts, will clean gilt frames. Vinegar rubbed over raw meat makes it tender.

Hot vinegar removes paint stains.

Vinegar and linseed oil in equal parts makes an excellent furniture polish.

Miss Gladys Roe, High Street.

To clean glass decanters and bedroom water bottles.

Glass decanters often get stained impossible to clean. The following method is easy and sure. Cover some egg shell with lemon juice, and let it stand 48 hours, when the egg shell will be quite dissolved. Pour it into the decanter and let it stand for a day, shaking occasionally, and then rinse with clean luke-warm water, when the decanter will be beautifully clear.

Mrs. Davies Hughes, Medical Hall.

Nutritious Coffee.

Dissolve a little in glass in boiling water. Put 1 oz of coffee with it in a saucepan, with a pint of milk which should be nearly boiling before the coffee is added. Boil all together for two minutes.

Mrs. Griffiths, Talafor.

Home-made Soap.

Clarify 4 lbs fat, put into an enamelled vessel large enough to allow free and constant stirring. Melt down (but don't let it get too hot). Put 1 lb caustic soda into 2 pints cold water, stir occasionally till quite cooled down, by which time the soda will be dissolved. Pour into fat, being careful to do so very slowly, and stir for exactly three minutes by the clock. Line a box with a piece of calico to prevent sticking, and pour into this. Put into a warm place for 24 hours covered with a folded blanket. Cut up and keep for four week when it will be ready for use.

Miss M.A. Evans, Rhianfa.

To Iron a Blouse.

The best way to iron a blouse. First iron the trimmings, then the collar and cuffs, then the yoke, and then the body, beginning with button side of front and with the top placed at the left hand. Iron from bottom to top right across blouse. Lastly iron sleeves.

Miss Sinah Hughes, Bron Eifion.

Washing without Hot Water.

Put garments in plain cold water to soak for about 2 hours. In some more cold water melt some washing soda or Rinso. Put the clothes in this and leave them again for some time. If you have not a washer then stir them about with your hands or a stick. Rinse out and put into cold blued water.

Miss K. Jones, High Street.

Bleaching.

Dissolve 1 lb washing soda in 1 quart boiling water, then add contents of 1 packet of chloride of lime and stir well. When cold pour off the clear solution and keep it in a well corked bottle. Use one teacupful of the solution to 2 quarts of cold water and leave the article in all night. It is wiser to wet thoroughly everything before putting in the solution to stand. Boil and wash as usual.

Mrs. Cybi Jones, Bryntirion Terrace.

To remove any stain.

Dissolve 1 lb soda in 1 quart boiling water, then stir in 1 ¼ lbs chloride of lime, and let it stand until cold. Strain very carefully and bottle. This is also used as a bleach. Put a small quantity in a tub of water, pour in the white clothes over night, and rinse, blue and dry in the usual way next day, and your clothes will look as if they had been grass bleached.

Mrs. Cybi Jones, Bryntirion Terrace.

To remove Perspiration Stains.

If a white blouse or any garment is stained under the arms, put it to soak for half an hour in warm water, to which a little ammonia has been added. Use no soap as it sets the stain. Then wring, and if the mark has not quite gone, squeeze a little lemon juice on to it and rinse in clean warm water. Afterwards wash in the usual way. I have found this most successful.

Mrs. Clifford Evans, Manafon, Pentrefelin

Sealing Bottles.

Plaster of Paris is an excellent material for sealing catchup and fruit bottles or jugs, and is more easily applied than sealing wax.

Miss Janie Griffith, Aberkin.

Furniture Cream.

Plaster of Paris is an excellent material for sealing catchup and fruit bottles or jugs, and is more easily applied than sealing wax.

Miss Janie Griffith, Aberkin.

A good Furniture Polish.

½ pint turpentine, ¼ pint raw linseed oil, ¼ pint methylated spirits. Shake well before using.

Mrs. Pritchard, Sheffield House.

To take out marks from Mahogany.

Rub in oil, and afterwards pour a little spirits of wine on the spot, afterwards rubbing it with a clean cloth. Then polish with furniture polish. This has been proved and is satisfactory.

Mrs. Davies, Bron Eifion Lodge.

To take hot plate mark out of polished table.

Take linseed oil and fine glass paper. Use abundance of oil and rub gently with a circular movement till stains disappear. Then polish with beeswax.

Mrs. Bartleman, Ymwlch.

DRINKS.

Gingerbeer, Westminster School.

3 oz cream of tartar, 4 ox ginger well bruised, 2 1bs loaf sugar, 18 cloves. The peel of 2 lemons. Boil three gallons of water, pour it while hot on the ingredients, let it stand, covered, till nearly cold, then add the juice of 2 lemons and 2 tablespoonfuls of yeast. Let it remain 12 hours. Then strain it through flannel, bottle it, and cork down strongly with string. This quantity makes three doz. bottles. It is fit to drink in a few days. Very good.

Mrs. Greaves, Bron Eifion.

Ginger Wine Essence.

2 drams of essence of cayenne, 3 drams of essence of ginger, ½ burnt sugar, 1 oz citric acid, 2 quarts boiling water. 3 lbs lump sugar. Put the sugar and other ingredients into a pan and pour the boiling water over. When cold bottle. For use, to half a wine glass of the essence fill up with hot or cold water, according to taste.

Mrs. Cambriensis Williams, Eryldon.

Lemonade.

Wash three lemons. Rub well over with lump sugar to extract the oil the skin. This gives a specially rich flavour not obtained by peeling. Squeeze the juice and pour one quart boiling water over, adding sugar to taste. Do not allow any pips or white skin as that makes it bitter.

Miss Leah E. Thomas, Mynydd Ednyfed.

61

Barley Water.

¼ lb pearl barley, 12 pieces lump sugar, the juice of 4 lemons. Thoroughly wash the barley, then put in pan with the required quantity of water. Add sugar and lemon, boil slowly until cooked. Then strain. Sufficient for six quarts.

Mrs. Drage, Parciau.

APPENDIX 1

Recipes of dishes which Lloyd George enjoyed,
given by

Mrs. Blodwen Evans.

BRAWN
a pig's head
1 lb beef
blade mace, cloves, bunch of herbs, salt and pepper

Thoroughly cleanse the head and put to soak all night. Rinse well and put in a saucepan with the beef, cover with water and bring to the boil. When at boiling point, remove scum. Add a blade of mace, 3 or 4 cloves, and a bunch of herbs. Simmer gently for about 2 ½ hours.

Strain the stock from the meat, reserve and allow to get cold. Remove fat from the jellied stock. Turn out the tongue, and skin, then cut into small pieces. Also cut all the meat from the head and the beef. Put into a bowl and add a little of the jellied stock. Add salt and pepper to your taste.

Have ready bowls and put the mixture in. Then put something flat over the bowls with a weight on top. When well pressed, turn out on a dish and garnish with parsley.

GRILLED HERRINGS
2 medium-sized fresh herrings, or 3 small ones
a small piece of butter
parsley
mustard sauce

Scale and clean the fish, then wipe with a clean cloth. Upon each side of the herrings cut three incisions 1 ½ ins. apart, cutting down to the backbone but not through it. Remove the heads. Now as the herrings contain their own cooking fat, grill quickly under a very hot grill till brown on each side. Dust lightly with salt, garnish with parsley and serve with mustard sauce.

CHEESE STRAWS
2 ozs flour
2 ozs grated cheese
salt, cayenne pepper
½ teaspoon mustard
yolk of an egg

Sift flour into a basin, add mustard, cayenne and grated cheese. Rub in butter, mix into a paste with the yolk of egg - add a little water if needed. Knead slightly.

Roll out on a pastry board to ⅛ of an inch thick, cut into narrow strips about 3 inches long. Place on a greased pastry tin and bake in a quick oven.

STEAMED SNOWDON PUDDING
¼ lb stale breadcrumbs
¾ oz ground rice of semolina
2 oz shredded suet or melted margarine
2 oz raisins
2 tablespoons golden syrup
3 oz castor sugar
1 egg
½ gill milk
2 tablespoons orange marmalade
grated rind of lemon or orange

Mix the crumbs with the ground rice or semolina. Stir in suet or margarine. Stone the raisins and place them in a greased pudding basin with 2 tablespoons golden syrup. Add sugar to crumb mixture. Beat till blended. Pour gently into the basin so as not to disturb the raisins, filling only three-quarters full.

Cover tightly with greased paper. Steam for 2 hours. Serve with custard or marmalade sauce. Serves three or four persons.

CACEN GRI (Dame Margaret's Way)
1 lb flour
6 oz butter
1 egg
a few currants
sugar to taste
1 teaspoonful baking powder and as much bicarbonate of soda as a sixpenny piece will hold.

Mix the baking powder and bicarb on your hand, then add to flour. Rub in the butter. Add the currants and sugar to taste. Beat the egg into the milk then beat well into the flour mixture. Roll out thinly and bake on a greased griddle.